Why p

Why Philosophize?

Jean-François Lyotard

Translated by Andrew Brown

polity

First published in *Pourquoi philosopher?* © Presses Universitaires de France, 2012

This English edition © Polity Press, 2013

Ouvrage publié avec le concours du Ministère Français chargé de la Culture – Centre National du Livre
Published with the assistance of the French Ministry of Culture – National Centre for the Book

Polity Press
65 Bridge Street
Cambridge CB2 1UR, UK

Polity Press
350 Main Street
Malden, MA 02148, USA

All rights reserved. Except for the quotation of short passages for the purpose of criticism and review, no part of this publication may be reproduced, stored in a retrieval system, or transmitted, in any form or by any means, electronic, mechanical, photocopying, recording or otherwise, without the prior permission of the publisher.

ISBN-13: 978-0-7456-7072-0 (hardback)
ISBN-13: 978-0-7456-7073-7 (paperback)

A catalogue record for this book is available from the British Library.

Typeset in 12.5 on 15 pt Adobe Garamond by
Servis Filmsetting Ltd, Stockport, Cheshire
Printed and bound in Great Britain by Clays Ltd, St Ives plc

The publisher has used its best endeavours to ensure that the URLs for external websites referred to in this book are correct and active at the time of going to press. However, the publisher has no responsibility for the websites and can make no guarantee that a site will remain live or that the content is or will remain appropriate.

Every effort has been made to trace all copyright holders, but if any have been inadvertently overlooked the publisher will be pleased to include any necessary credits in any subsequent reprint or edition.

For further information on Polity, visit our website: www.politybooks.com

Contents

Acknowledgements vi

Editorial note vii

Introduction 1

1 Why desire? 17

2 Philosophy and origin 44

3 On philosophical speech 70

4 On philosophy and action 100

Acknowledgements

The publisher wishes to thank Dolorès Lyotard and Corinne Enaudeau, as well as the team of the Bibliothèque littéraire Jacques Doucet (especially Marie-Dominique Nobécourt Mutarelli, the Head Librarian), for their generous help in preparing this edition. Corinne Enaudeau teaches philosophy to *khâgne* and *hypokhâgne* classes at the Janson de Sailly and Henri IV lycées in Paris.

Editorial note

The translation follows a typed text preserved at the Bibliothèque littéraire Jacques Doucet (shelf mark JFL 291/2). This constitutes the second manuscript version of the lectures given by Jean-François Lyotard soon after they had been written. The Bibliothèque Doucet also preserves (shelf mark JFL 291/1) a first typewritten version of the same text – but one that is heavily annotated by Lyotard himself. All these annotations have been carried over, without modification or alteration, into the second typescript, so it has not been thought useful to point out the differences between the two versions. On the other hand, a few minor corrections have been made when they turned out to be necessary (punctuation mistakes, quotation marks missing); likewise, the quotations indicated by abbreviated references in the original text have been re-established. No notes have been added, so as to leave the oral character of these lectures intact.[1]

Corinne Enaudeau

---

[1] I have added a minimum of notes where I felt they were necessary. [Trans. note]

Introduction

Corinne Enaudeau

Philosophy does not desire wisdom or knowledge; it teaches us neither what is true nor how to behave. People will say that it wears itself out wondering what it is – and *what is* – in a solitude that disturbs nobody. At best, it might sometimes offer us an idea useful for the production of wealth or the dream of a completely different social system or the metaphysical opium of consolation. Philosophers, it would seem, are those crazy chatterboxes whom history carts along with it throughout its history, without profit but without any great loss either. They may well interpret the world, but they stay standing at its door and will never change it. So their discourse may be interrupted, may return to silence, without the face of the world being changed. After all, their discourse has, in the final analysis, a single thread: a strange attachment to loss, the desire not to lose the loss that undermines all human activity and separates it from itself, the desire not to let go of the lack whose dagger death sticks into life. So, in 2012, we may well ask, as Jean-François Lyotard asked in 1964: why philosophize? What reason was there, is there still, to philosophize, to plunge back down into the depths of the gaps in meaning – each time anew, in a re-found naivety that will be judged childish? Put this way, the question may appear rhetorical. It is self-referential, since its utterance actually gives the answer to the question uttered, for we have already started philosophizing when we wonder whether it's worth the trouble to do so all over again. But it is the lot of language itself, which has to speak so as to worry about its own interruption; it is the lot of wakefulness and life, which must deny in practice the sleep and death that they are investigating. Since we speak, act and live under the threat of loss, we won't emerge from this circle where absence makes itself present and presence is hollowed out by absence. For it is not easy to be a dumb beast, Lyotard tells us, we cannot stun ourselves with a wordless given, a perfect plenitude, a dreamless night. So we will philosophize for the simple reason that we cannot avoid doing so: 'attest to the presence of lack by our speech'.

The man who died in 1998, leaving *The Confession of Augustine* unfinished, was perhaps preoccupied by nothing other than this constitutive incompleteness of meaning, which is the knife and the wound of thought, its burning sore and its viaticum. *Discourse, figure* declared that it refused to conclude, *The Differend* interrupted its succession of paragraphs with a few abrupt items on history. Each of Lyotard's books brings a certain disjunction into its object, into its writing, into the gap between it and the other books. His conviction, as early as 1964, was that you can be inoculated with a grain of philosophy only if you let yourself be haunted by absence and find the paradoxical energy to contaminate others with it, to tell them about the 'law of debt', the debit that can never be paid off. His work enabled this grain to spread and grow, but in Lyotard it was accompanied by a vigorous engagement with teaching, and a political commitment in which questioning, professing, and leading the life of an activist went inseparably together. Attention to the flaw – to the lack of substantiality as much as of meaning – already presupposes that it is other people, even more than things, who make holes in language; that it is through others that unity is lacking in the social totality, through them that opposition comes to split open the unity of meaning. Without them being there to muddle arguments, thwart actions, disappoint passions, lack would never come to the real to turn it into a human world, and this world would not call on speech to reflect its lack, to philosophize. If, however, it is simply a matter of filling an empty space, philosophy can easily build a non-human world in it, a harmonious metaphysical dream. It then encloses itself within an absolute Logos, the mirage of an invisible Whole that paradoxically remains separate from what it unites. Ideology is simply this, says Lyotard – a system of ideas that is all the more easy to profess in that it is autonomous, has sublimated the lack from which it has sprung, and speaks elsewhere, beyond. This is true of all metaphysics, but also of all theory, even if it calls itself Marxist, which attempts to fill needy minds with its overflow of system. 'To cut oneself away from practice' doesn't mean talking about substance instead of working for revolution, it means turning both of them into the solution, maintaining that the end is in the beginning, that meaning has always belonged to itself, that it knows where it is and where it is going. For the voice that utters this meaning can no longer capture any of the silent disunions in which, however, this meaning seeks itself. To profess – at least to profess philosophy, not faith or science – is nothing without the questions that we ask ourselves and ask others, without this shared commerce of lack in which a 'paradoxical power of passivity' (a recurrent theme in Lyotard's whole work) is exercised, the power to allow the world to come into speech, to allow ourselves to be told what is lacking in the real for it to be a picture, and what is lacking in the picture for it to be real.

This is how Lyotard taught, telling his students and listeners that they would learn nothing from him unless they learned to unlearn, as he said again at Nanterre in 1984 (in a lecture published in *The post-modern explained to children*). But in 1964, at the age of forty, he himself already had to start unlearning what he thought he had learnt, to break away from an activist orthodoxy that had indeed taught him to unlearn metaphysics, but had taught him to hope for revolution and, with it, a resolution to history. Letting go of revolutionary teleology without losing the loss that, however crushed, was attested in it – the absolute lack or 'general wrong' known as exploitation – meant knowing that he would need to speak the ambiguous language of yes and no, presence and absence, in other words to correct Marxism with Freud, historical materialism with the ambivalence of the drives, social reconciliation with the uncertainty of desire. In short, he would need to restore to Marx's voice the strength of which Hegelian totalization had deprived it, the strength to express separation: the separation of society from itself, the separation of world from mind, of reality from meaning. But also, in Freud's view, the separation of love from its object, of one sex from the other, of childhood from language. All these divisions were labelled 'oppositions' in 1964: in *Discourse, figure*, they would be shunted off in favour of 'differences' and later radicalized as irreducible 'differends': the differend between employees and capital, as ever, but also – albeit in a very different way – between Judaism and Christianity. 'Childhood' would remain the name Lyotard used to re-think, for over thirty years, the exposure to a brutal emotion that saps language and yet demands it.

For now, in 1964, he needed to start over again without knowing quite how to begin, since childhood is, within man, what 'throws him off course [*son dé-cours*] [. . .] the possibility or risk of being adrift' (in the words of 1984). Lyotard began his 'Dérive à partir de Marx et Freud' ('Drifting away from Marx and Freud') at the point he had reached, 'mid-course' (*en cours*), in the middle of his path and the middle of his philosophy course, between the Sorbonne where he taught, 'Socialisme ou barbarie' and later 'Pouvoir ouvrier' where he was still active (for a short period), his short introductory book on phenomenology in the encyclopaedic 'Que Sais-Je?' series published in 1954, Lacan's seminar where he learnt to read Freud, and Culioli's seminar where he gained a grounding in linguistics. It was from amidst all of this that he tried to make audible to his students the loss of unity, and to hollow out, in himself as in them, a sense of mourning for lost completeness and a place in which to anchor the philosopher's responsibility.

Philosophical discourse is driven by a contradictory passion. For its desire to possess itself in an absolutely isolated state comes with the wish not to possess itself, to remain a language immersed in the world and dependent on its deficiency. To teach philosophy means to put this ambiguity to work. But the operation would have a disappointing, didactic effect – disappointing *because* didactic – only if the 'course' of and in philosophy is mid-course, if it begins in the middle, at the point where the interlocutors have arrived with their history and their questions. So it is an extra-curricular course, a course outside any preparatory genealogy, a course that is neither in the world (from which the question separates it) nor outside the world (in a speech spoken already elsewhere), but to the world, in that distance where, as Lyotard says, we allow ourselves to be penetrated by the thing at the same time as we keep it at a distance so as to be able to judge it. Without this 'passibility' (a term he used in 1987) to the world, to the human world, that is, to its tenaciously present lack, teaching is merely a display of glittering jewellery, no doubt admirable but with nothing really at issue in it. This issue presupposes a tension between desire and responsibility. 'Philosophy has no particular desire [. . .] it is desire that has philosophy in the same way that it has absolutely anyone' – apart from the fact, adds Lyotard, that it turns round on this impulse that takes hold of it, and all human activity with it. But if it is satisfied by this reflection on desire, thought will have still have missed its debt.

For Lyotard in 1964, philosophy was still a praxis, just as psychoanalysis was, for Freud, also a clinical activity. The important thing was what social life lacked, not to reconcile itself with itself but to justify itself. The 'absolute lack', whose structure Marx revealed and called the 'proletariat', could indeed be intolerable but it did not indicate 'what society really desired', contrary to what official Marxism claimed. So we needed to give the opacity of this desire its due, and to sojourn in its silence; we had to endeavour to make explicit the latent, tacit meaning already there, hanging around in the relations between human beings. If Lyotard devotes the last of the four lectures to 'philosophy and action', this is because philosophical responsibility toward the lack is inseparable from the political debt toward the world: responsibility and debt together maintain the wager of converting silence into speech, passivity into action.

There are two simultaneous convictions at work here. The one, inherited from Husserl via Merleau-Ponty, is that the philosopher induces mute experience to express its own meaning. The other conviction, inherited from Marx, is that the philosopher interprets the world only to help change it. The two convictions respectively are discussed in detail in the third lecture on speech and the fourth on action. The first lecture, devoted to desire, inherits from Freud, via Lacan, the idea that any relation to presence is achieved against a background of absence. The second shows how desire is linked to language and action, and discusses the loss of unity and the preservation of this loss in the history, forever starting over again, of the philosophical effort. Presented in the right order, the treatment of the question 'why philosophize?' thus unfolds like this: the reason for philosophizing is that we desire, and that desire is accompanied by its questioning of its own movement. The reason for this reflection is that unity has been lost, not in some original disappearance that has made us forget unity itself, but in the unfolding of a history in which the fit between reality and meaning is always elusive and has to be tried out again and again, only to be lost again.

INTRODUCTION

The fact remains that we would not philosophize if we did not speak, and we would not speak if we could not say anything, if the silence of the world condemned discourse to ramble, or if a logos immanent to the world had already said everything and doomed words to do nothing but repeat it. It is 'childhood through which the world holds onto us', the wound of being grasped by the world, which makes the philosopher speak, and gives him the 'passive strength that can attest to a meaning already there', a fragmentary meaning that makes his discourse incomplete and thus true. Because the world encroaches on us, speech can encroach on the world by expressing it, and action by changing it. We philosophize because we are exposed to the world and have the 'responsibility of naming what needs to be said and done'.

If philosophizing means allowing us to be taken over by a lack to which we attest without satisfying that lack, if teaching means making clear what we do not understand ourselves, the lesson is here magisterial, even in the way Lyotard handles paradoxes: the methodical transgression of the boundaries between the spheres of life and between different disciplines here serves to knot together desire, time, language and action, at an invisible boundary between presence and absence. The lesson is perhaps *too* magisterial if we remember the fragmentation that will be enacted in *Discourse, figure* seven years later, as well as Lyotard's subsequent work: from this viewpoint, the careful construction of 1964 still makes desire too happy, language too bodily, time too unified and action too enthusiastic. The death haunting life would soon no longer be able to acclimatize itself in lack, or curb itself in the faith in a latent meaning, it would make itself more trenchant in its de-structuring of the 'figural' or in the asphyxiated voice that seals 'the differend'. Whatever revisions were to follow, they were justified in advance because 'there is more than one philosopher – Plato, to begin with, or Kant, or Husserl – who in the course of his life performs this critique, turns round on what he has thought, undoes it and starts all over again, thus proving that the true unity of his work resides in the desire that stems from the loss of unity, and not a complacent acceptance of the fully formed system, the unity regained.' That the new beginning never started from scratch, contrary to what is said here, and that naivety is an exorbitant wish, is something that Lyotard was to show later in the very idea of revolution. His debate with historians, and his repeated analysis of time, showed that in relating history (whatever history it may be), we remain stuck with a spinning wheel that threatens either to get out of control and undo our work, or else to create a repressive web. Doubtless philosophy here finds material with which to question its own language, to seek its own rule and, as Lyotard says here, 'to irritate everybody'.

Why Philosophize?

Four lectures given to first-year students at the Sorbonne (October–November 1964)[1]

[1] Strictly speaking, these lectures were given to students in 'Propédeutique', an intermediate year of study at the beginning of a degree in an arts or sciences subject.

I

Why desire?

As you know, philosophers are in the habit of starting their courses with an examination of the question 'what is philosophy?' Every year, in all the institutions where it is taught as an established subject, the people responsible for philosophy ask themselves 'well, where is it? what kind of thing is it?'

Among the class of actes manqués, Freud includes not being able to put your hands on something that you know you have put away somewhere. The opening lecture of philosophers, a lecture they give again and again, is just like an acte manqué. Philosophy misses itself (*la philosophie se manque elle-même*), it is out of order, we set off to look for it from scratch, we are forever forgetting it, forgetting where it is. It appears and it disappears; it conceals itself. An acte manqué, too, is the concealment of an object or a situation from consciousness, an interruption in the weft of everyday life, a discontinuity.

When we ask ourselves not 'what is philosophy?' but '*why* philosophize?', we are emphasizing how discontinuous with itself philosophy is – how it is possible for philosophy to be absent. For most people, for most of you, philosophy is absent from their preoccupations, their studies, their lives. And for the philosopher himself, even if philosophy constantly needs to be recalled and re-established, this is because it sinks, because it slips between his fingers, because it goes under. So why philosophize rather than *not* philosophize? The interrogative adverb *pourquoi?* (*why?*) at least designates in the word *pour* (*for*) from which it is made a number of nuances of complement or attribute; but these nuances are all engulfed in the same hole, the hole drilled by the interrogative value of the adverb. This endows the thing under question with a surprising status: this thing might not be what it is, or might not be *tout court*. '*Pourquoi*' bears within itself the annihilation of what it is questioning. In this question we find the real presence of the thing that is being questioned (we take philosophy to be a fact, a reality) and its possible absence, we find both the life and death of philosophy, we have it and we do not have it.

Well, perhaps the secret of philosophy's existence lies precisely in this contradictory, contrasting situation. To grasp this potential relationship between the act of philosophizing and the 'presence–absence' structure, it will be useful to examine, even if only rapidly, what *desire* is. After all, in philosophy there is *philein*, to love, to be in love, to desire.

I would like to suggest just two themes that concern desire:

(1) We have fallen into the habit – as has philosophy itself, insofar as it accepts a certain way of asking questions – of examining a problem such as desire from the point of view of subject and object, the point of view of the duality between what desires and what is desired. As a result, the question of desire soon becomes the question of knowing whether it is the desirable that arouses desire or the complete opposite, with desire creating the desirable – whether you fall in love with a woman because she is lovable, or whether she

is lovable because you have fallen in love with her. We need to realize that this way of asking the question falls within the category of causality (the desirable would be the cause of desire, or vice versa), that it belongs to a dualist vision of things (on the one side there is the subject, and on the other the object, each endowed with its respective properties), and that it thereby makes any serious approach to the question impossible. Desire does not establish a relationship between a cause and an effect, of whatever kind they may be; desire, rather, is the movement of something that goes out toward the other as toward something that it itself lacks. This means that the *other* (the object, if you like – but is it the apparently desired object that is actually desired?) is present to what desires, and is present in the form of absence. That which desires has got what it lacks, without which it would not desire it, and yet it does not have it, it does not know it, otherwise it would not desire it either. So, going back to the concepts of subject and object, the movement of desire makes the apparent object appear as something that is already there in desire without however being there 'in flesh and blood', and the apparent subject appears as something indefinite, incomplete, which needs the other to define it, to complete it, something that is defined by the other, by absence. So on both sides there is the same contradictory but symmetrical structure: in the 'subject', the absence of what is desired, its lack, at the centre of its own presence, a certain non-being in the being which desires, and in the 'object' a presence, the presence to the desirer (memory, hope) against a background of absence, since the object is there as desired and ipso facto as possessed.

(2) From this stems our second theme. The essence of desire resides in this structure that combines presence and absence. The combination is not accidental. It is because what is present is absent from itself, or the absent present, that desire exists. Desire is really raised into being, set up by the absence of presence, or vice versa; something that is there is not there and wants to be there, wants to coincide with itself, to realize itself, and desire is simply that force that holds presence and absence together without mixing them up.

In the *Symposium*, Socrates tells of how a priestess from Mantinea, Diotima, described the birth of love, Eros, to him in these terms:

'The tale', she said, 'will take time; nevertheless I will tell you. On the birthday of Aphrodite there was a feast of the gods, at which the god Poros or Plenty, who is the son of Metis or Discretion, was one of the guests. When the feast was over, Penia or Poverty, as the manner is on such occasions, came about the doors to beg. Now Plenty, who was the worse for nectar (there was no wine in those days), went into the garden of Zeus and fell into a heavy sleep; and Poverty considering her own straitened circumstances, plotted to have a child by him, and accordingly she lay down at his side and conceived Love, who partly because he is naturally a lover of the beautiful, and because Aphrodite is herself beautiful, and also because he was born on her birthday, is her follower and attendant.'

(*Symposium* 203 b-c, trans. Jowett)

The condition of Eros or Love, his fate, clearly results from his heredity, if we are to believe Diotima:

'And as his parentage is, so also are his fortunes. In the first place he is always poor, and anything but tender and fair, as the many imagine him; and he is rough and squalid, and has no shoes, nor a house to dwell in; on the bare earth exposed he lies under the open heaven, in the streets, or at the doors of houses, taking his rest; and like his mother he is always in distress. Like his father too, whom he also partly resembles, he is always plotting against the fair and good; he is bold, enterprising, strong, a mighty hunter, always weaving some intrigue or other, keen in the pursuit of wisdom, fertile in resources; a philosopher at all times, terrible as an enchanter, sorcerer, sophist. He is by nature neither mortal nor immortal, but alive and flourishing at one moment when he is in plenty, and dead at another moment, and again alive by reason of his father's nature. But that which is always flowing in is always flowing out, and so he is never in want and never in wealth [. . .].'

(*Symposium* 203 c-e)

Diotima's story, the myth of the birth of Eros, certainly generates many reflections. We can, at least, pick out the following ideas:

– first, the theme of Eros being conceived on the same day that Aphrodite or Beauty – his object, in short – comes into the world; there is a sort of knowledge of desire and the desirable;

– second, the idea that Eros has a twofold nature; he is not a god, he is not a man, he participates in the divine through his father who was at the table of the gods and was overwhelmed by (got drunk on) the divine intoxication of nectar, he is mortal on his mother's side – she is a beggar and cannot be self-sufficient. Thus there is life and death, and Plato insists on the alternating of life and death in the life of Eros. He is like the Phoenix: 'Die at dusk he may, but then / The Morning sees him born again' (Apollinaire, 'Chanson du Mal-Aimé' ('Song of the Unloved'), *Alcools*). We can even go a little further: it is because desire is in straitened circumstances that it needs to be ingenious, while its inventions always eventually fail. This means that Eros remains under the law of Death, of Poverty, he constantly needs to escape it, to reinvent his life, precisely because he bears death within him;

– finally, desire is man and woman at the same time as life and death. This means that, in Plato's text, the contrasting pair life–death is, to at least some extent, identified with the contrasting pair male–female. The father of Eros symbolizes what, within desire, brings love closer to its object, their reunion, while his mother, poverty, embodies what keeps them apart. In this text, attraction is virile, and repulsion is feminine. We cannot go into this right now, but we at least need to remember that however much Eros may be of the male sex, he is in reality man and woman.

In a paper read out to the French Society for Psychoanalysis (published in May 1965, in *La Psychanalyse*, 2, pp. 139 ff.), Serge Leclaire, a disciple of Dr Jacques Lacan, characterized the symptom of hysteria by the unformulated question, 'Am I am man or a woman?', while in his view the symptom of obsession consists rather in the question, 'Am I dead or alive?'

So we find the same, twofold ambiguity in the modern interpretation of neuroses that Diotima scrutinized in Eros: the ambiguity of life and of sex. Illness sheds a revealing light on this uncertainty: a person who is ill does not know which side to categorize himself in, whether to place himself in life or in death, in virility or in femininity. And the revelation that illness provides is not only proof of how much Plato is still of concern to us, of how greatly Freudian investigations echo the central problems of philosophy: it shows us that the *yes and no*, the contrasting pair, as Leclaire puts it – a pair whose poles are kept apart in neurosis – rules our lives (and not only our love lives); that even when we are at the heart of things, of ourselves, of others, of time or of speech, their reverse side is constantly present to us: 'All relationship to presence is achieved against a background of absence' (Lacan). Thus desire, which essentially contains this opposition in its conjunction, is our Master.

Do we still have to ask ourselves what we need to understand by desire, and what we are talking about when we talk about desire?

You will have already realized that we still need to get rid of the current idea, the stereotype, that there is a sphere of Eros, of sexuality, which lies apart from the others – that we have an emotional life with its specific problems, an economic life with *its* problems, an intellectual life devoted to speculative questions, etc. This idea, to be sure, is not entirely baseless, and we'll try to explain this issue in more detail later. But if, for example, Freud's work has had and continues to have the impact that you are aware of, this is definitely not because he put sexuality everywhere, something which would hardly be any more illuminating than putting the economy everywhere, as certain Marxists do. It is, rather, because Freud embarked on forging a link between sexual life and emotional life, social life, and religious life, and brought sexual life out of its ghetto – not by reducing other activities to the libido, but by investigating in depth the structure of behaviour and by beginning to reveal a symbolic pattern that is perhaps common to all of them.

Staying with our theme, the relationship of desire to the contrast between attraction and repulsion, we could find many examples to illustrate it. For example, sticking very close to the theme of Eros, to begin with, and to appeal to the more literary among you, what Proust narrates in *The Fugitive* is desire, but with a particular spin, for desire at the moment of its waning is Eros as the son of Poverty, the weight of death in desire; what Proust describes and analyses is the paroxysm of separation, an intensified separation. There is the separation caused by the death of Albertine, and then there is the separation stemming from Marcel's jealousy that came between him and the young woman while she was still alive. Albertine's death gives a particular form to desire, namely mourning; but her death does not suppress desire since jealousy continues to cast its suspicion on the dead woman. And jealousy is itself a kind of putting to death of the living woman, in that it sets her presence aside. Behind the present woman, I see *the same woman as other*; I annihilate her presence and I forge the image of her that I do not know. The absence that was already the absence of Albertine present, because of Marcel's suspicions, is intensified by the absence resulting from death, an absence maintained by the young woman's persistent presence...

This, if you like, is an immediate illustration of desire, an accessible example of it. But it is clear that the whole work, the whole of *In Search of Lost Time*, is bathed in the same twilit glow; it is not just a woman whom you fail to possess in flesh and blood, it is also a society falling apart, other people rendered unrecognizable by age, and, first and foremost, time, which scatters its moments rather than holding them together. Let's leave the twilight, the lesson that Proust probably wants to teach us in his book, and let's take up one of these themes that the more historically minded of you may well find interesting:

the idea that history and society also contain an alternation of attraction and repulsion, and that they thus stem from desire.

It is not too venturesome to read the history of the West at least as the contradictory movement in which the set of different social units (*individuals*, or *groups*, for example social classes), seeks and fails to find unity with itself. This history has been marked hitherto by the alternation, within societies and between them, of dispersal and unification, and this alternation is profoundly homologous with that of desire. Eros needs all the ingenuity he has inherited from the gods on his father's side if he is not to fall into poverty. Likewise, civilization is threatened by death, namely a poverty of values, and society is threatened by discontinuity, by an interruption of the communication between its parts: hence nothing is settled once and for all, and both civilization and society constantly need to be grasped afresh, and remade with the dynamism that, as Diotima says of the son of Poros, strives forward with all its strength. We ourselves, as sociality and historicity, also live against a background of death and we also belong to desire. So it needs to be clear that, by the word 'desire', we mean the relationship that simultaneously unites and separates its terms, makes them exist within each other as well as outside of each other.

I think that we can now get back to philosophy and grasp how philosophy is *philein*, love, by testing out on it the two characteristics that we have analysed in relation to desire.

At the end of the *Symposium*, the drunken Alcibiades (and as he himself puts it, truth lies in wine) delivers a speech in praise of Socrates, next to whom he is reclining. Of this portrait, one fragment deserves our attention, since we are trying to understand why we should philosophize; it is the passage where Alcibiades tells the following story. Convinced that Socrates is in love with him, since the philosopher eagerly seeks out the company of handsome young men, he decides to give him an opportunity to yield to temptation. Faced with this opportunity, Socrates then explains their situation to him in the following way: basically, says Socrates, you feel that you have found in me a beauty even more extraordinary than your own, a beauty of another order, a hidden, spiritual beauty; and you want to swap them, you want to give me your beauty and receive mine in exchange; this would be a real bargain for you, if at least I was really in possession of that hidden beauty that you suspect. But this is not certain; we need to think it over together. Alcibiades believes that Socrates has accepted the deal, he throws a cloak over him and slips in next to him. But all night long, Alcibiades relates, nothing happens – nothing more extraordinary than if he had been sleeping on 'the couch of a father or an elder brother'. And Alcibiades adds:

> And therefore I could not be angry with him or renounce his company, any more than I could hope to win him. [. . .] So I was at my wit's end; no one was ever more hopelessly enslaved by another.
>
> (*Symposium* 219 d-e)

In this story, Alcibiades is reporting on a game, the game of desire, and he reveals to us with a sophisticated innocence the philosopher's position in this game. Let's take a closer look at this.

Alcibiades thinks that Socrates is in love with him, but he himself desires to obtain from Socrates 'that [he] will assist [Alcibiades] in the way of virtue', teach him everything (217a). Alcibiades proposes an exchange: he will grant his favours to Socrates, and Socrates will repay him with his wisdom.

Assailed by this strategy, what will Socrates do? He seeks to neutralize it, and – as we shall see – his reply remains really quite ambiguous.

Socrates does not turn down Alcibiades' proposal, he does not refute his argument. There is no sarcastic banter about the – necessarily somewhat presumptuous – hypothesis that Socrates is in love with Alcibiades; no indignation about the planned exchange; barely a hint of irony touching Alcibiades' business sense.

What Socrates does is simply question this wonderful bargain and ask himself aloud what is so wonderful about it: that is all. Alcibiades wants to exchange something visible, his beauty, against something invisible, Socrates' wisdom. He is running a big risk: maybe he will obtain nothing in exchange for his favours, if there is not any wisdom there. This wonderful bargain is a wager, not double or quits, but at best quits, at worst a dead loss. It's risky.

You can see it is just as if Socrates were picking up Alcibiades' cards after laying his own on the table, and showing him that they do not mean he can definitely win. The situation is not a cash market, but a credit market in which the debtor – here, Socrates – is not sure of being creditworthy. Socrates has laid his hand of cards on the table, but in fact he does not have any real cards to play. In relation to Alcibiades' strategy, nothing further can occur, since this strategy rested on the exchange of beauty against wisdom, and Socrates states that he is not sure he can keep his side of the bargain. But Alcibiades interprets this statement as a feint and this is why he reiterates – in deeds, this time, rather than in words – his first proposal. But it is not a lover he finds under the cloak but, as he says himself, a father! So Socrates is left to wait and see, and Alcibiades is left in error.

We can see that Alcibiades remains in error until the end of his narrative, when he again interprets Socrates' attitude as a strategy superior to his own: he wanted to vanquish the philosopher, but he is vanquished; he wanted to dominate him (since he would be in possession of his own beauty *and* of the wisdom won from Socrates), but he ends up being his slave. Socrates has outsmarted him, he has caught him out; the roles that Alcibiades attributed to Socrates and himself at the beginning of the game are now reversed: the lover is no longer Socrates, but Alcibiades.

We might even say that, by presenting the story this way in the presence of Socrates, even though he is reclining right next to Socrates, as was already the case on the night he is narrating, he is merely repeating the same confused ploy that drove him to make his initial proposal; he is going a bit further, but he is still persisting in the same strategy; he gets Socrates to understand that he is completely vanquished, defenceless, and thus runs no danger, so that really this time Socrates has nothing to fear, and everything to gain by going through with the deal; he is like the carpet seller running after the buyer who will not offer any more than 50,000, and telling him, 'Listen, I'm giving it away, I'll let you have it for a mere 55,000.'

But though this comparison offers itself spontaneously, it does force us to think: is it really a mistake, an aberration on Alcibiades' part? Or is it rather that, by reiterating the first procedure, Alcibiades is thwarting the Socratic game? After all, the slave is the master of the master (Hegel). And it is the best way of playing – the best play of passion – that if it cannot get what it wants by taking, it conquers by giving itself. In fact, Alcibiades plays his game and, in his own way, he plays it well. For ultimately, Socrates is checked, he has not managed to persuade Alcibiades to accept the neutralization that he was offering.

So what does the philosopher want? When he states that he is not sure he possesses wisdom, is this merely so that he can bind Alcibiades all the more securely to him? Is Socrates just a more sophisticated seducer, a more subtle player who falls in with the other's logic and sets up a trap for him by feigning to be weak? This is what Alcibiades believes, and this is what Alcibiades himself, as we have just said, tries to do. This is also what the Athenians will believe: they will not let themselves be convinced that Socrates' only aim is to question them about their activities, their virtues, their religion and their city, and they will suspect him of surreptitiously introducing new gods into Athens. So they will condemn him to death.

Socrates knows full well what other people believe, Alcibiades first and foremost; but he does not think that he himself is a better player. Stating as he does that he lacks wisdom is no feint as far as he is concerned. Quite the contrary: it is the hypothesis of the feint that proves how much he does lack wisdom, since it presupposes, in its naive stratagem, that the philosopher really is wise and that he is saying the opposite the better to intrigue (in both senses of the word). Now believing that Socrates has wisdom to exchange, wisdom for sale, is precisely the madness that he is attacking.

For Socrates, the neutralization of Alcibiades' logic is the sole aim in view; for this neutralization would, if it succeeded, mean that Alcibiades has realized that wisdom is not the object of an exchange, not because it is too precious for anyone to find an equivalent to swop, but because it is never sure of itself, is always lost and always needs to be found again, the presence of an absence, especially because it is itself an awareness of the exchange, a fully aware exchange, an awareness that there is no object, but only an exchange. Socrates seeks to trigger this reflection by suspending Alcibiades' logic, which takes wisdom to be a having, to be a thing, a *res*, the reifying logic of Alcibiades and also of the Athenians.

But he cannot break off the conversation there, withdraw from the community and the game, because he needs this absence to be recognized by others. Socrates knows perfectly well that to be right all alone against all the others is not to be right but to be wrong, to be crazy. By opening up his own emptiness, his own vacancy when faced with Alcibiades' onslaught, he wants to hollow out the same emptiness in Alcibiades too; by telling his accusers that his whole wisdom consists in knowing that he knows nothing, he wants to trigger yet further reflection. And in my view, we have sufficient proof that this is indeed Socrates' logic, the way he plays his own game by playing along with others: the proof is that he agrees to drink the hemlock; for if he had not disconcerted his adversary so as to better him and master him, he would not have agreed to die. By dying willingly, he is suggesting to them that he really did have nothing to lose, that there was nothing behind his stratagem.

What the philosopher desires is not that different desires be convinced and conquered, but that they be inflected and reflected. By saying that he knows that he does not know, while the others do not know and think they know and grasp things, and by dying for this, he wants to show that there is in demand – in Alcibiades' demand, for example – more than what it demands, and this more is a less, a nothing at all. The very possibility of desire, he shows, actually means the presence of an absence, and perhaps the whole of wisdom consists in opening our ears to this absence and tarrying with it. Instead of seeking wisdom – a mad quest – Alcibiades would do better (as would you and I) to wonder why he is seeking. To philosophize is not to desire wisdom, it is to desire desire . . . This is why the path on which Alcibiades is set, having been thrown off course, leads nowhere, it is a *Holzweg*, as Heidegger would put it, 'the trail left up to the edge of the forest by the wood which the woodcutter brings back from it'. Follow this trail back: it will shake you off while leading to the heart of the forest.

This does not mean that Socrates was not in love; as I have said, not once does he deny that Alcibiades' beauty is desirable. He in no way advocates disengagement from the passions, abstinence or abstraction far from the world. On the contrary, there is love in philosophy; it is its resource, its expedient. But philosophy is within love as its Poverty.

Philosophy has no particular desire; it is not a speculation on a separate theme or in a

WHY DESIRE?

separate domain. Philosophy has the same passions as everyone, she is the daughter of her time, as Hegel says. But I think it would be easier to agree with what has been shown if we first said: it is desire that has philosophy in the same way that it has absolutely anyone ... The philosopher is not some fine fellow who wakes up and says to himself, 'They've forgotten to think about God, or history, or space, or being; I need to see to this!' Such a situation would mean that the philosopher is the inventor of his problems, and if this were true, nobody would recognize himself, would recognize any substance, in what the philosopher might have to say. Now even if the link from philosophical discourse to what has been happening in the world for centuries is not immediately clear, we all know that Socratic irony, Platonic dialogue, Cartesian meditation, Kantian critique, Hegelian dialectic, and the Marxist movement have continually determined our fate and are there, folded down on top of each other, in thick strata, in the soil of our present culture; we know that each of these modes of philosophical speech has been a moment when the West sought to say itself and understand itself in its discourse; we know that this speech about itself, this distance from itself is not superfluous, added on, secondary in relation to the civilization of the West, but is on the contrary its core, its difference; and finally we know that these past philosophies are not abolished, because we continue to hear them and respond to them.

Philosophers do not invent their problems, they are not mad, at least in the sense of talking to themselves. They may be mad, perhaps, but if so, no more than anyone else, in the other sense that 'it wants [*ça veut*] through them', that they are possessed, inhabited by the yes and no. It is the movement of desire which, yet again, holds together what is separate or keeps apart things that go together, it is this movement that runs through philosophy, it is by opening up to it and in order to open up to it that we philosophize. We can yield to movement in very different ways: we can be susceptible to the fact that two and two makes four, or that a man and a woman make a couple, or that a multitude of individuals makes a society or that a host of instants makes a duration, or that a succession of words makes a meaning, or that a series of actions makes a life – and at the same time we realize that none of these results can be taken for granted, that the unity of

WHY DESIRE?

the couple or of time, of language or of number remains immersed in the elements that form it, and is dependent on their fate. In short, philosophy can swoop down on us from any point of the compass.

So there is no desire proper to the philosopher; as Alain used to say, 'For philosophy, any subject is good, so long as it is foreign!' But there is a way of encountering desire that is particular to the philosopher. This particularity, as we now know it, is that with philosophy, desire is inflected, it reflects itself, it desires itself. And then it raises the question: why desire? Why does what is two seek to make one, and why does what is one need the other? Why is unity spread out in multiplicity and why does multiplicity depend on unity? Why is unity always given in separation? Why is there not just unity, immediate unity, but always the mediation of the one through the other? Why is the opposition that both separates and unites the master of all?

So the answer to the question, 'Why philosophize?' lies in the ineluctable question, 'Why desire?' The desire comprised by philosophy is no less uncontrollable than any desire, but it becomes doubly intense, questioning itself in its very movement. In any case, it is not from reality alone that philosophy aims its questions towards things; and in my view, this immanence of philosophizing to desiring appears in the very origin of the word, if we pay attention to the root of the term *sophia*: the root *soph-* is the same as the root of the Latin *sap-*, *sapere*, and of the French '*savoir*' ('to know') and '*savourer*' ('to savour'). Whatever is *sophon* knows how to savour; and savouring presupposes both that the thing can be tasted and that it is at a distance; we allow ourselves to be penetrated by the thing, we mingle with it, and at the same time we keep it at bay, so as to be able to say it, to judge it. We keep it in the outside of the inside, namely in our mouths (which are also the place of speech). To philosophize is fully to obey the movement of desire, to be included within it, and at the same time to try and understand it without leaving one's own path.

So it is no coincidence if the earliest Greek philosophy, the philosophers curiously known as the pre-Socratics, rather as the Toltecs, the Aztecs and the Incas are known as pre-Columbians, as if Socrates had discovered the continent of philosophy and as if people had realized that this continent was already occupied by thoughts filled with power and magnificence (as Montaigne said of the Indian capitals, Cuzco and Mexico), it is thus no coincidence that this entire early philosophy, which may not be a philosophy in Socrates' sense or ours, is haunted by the question of the one and the many, which is the question of desire, as well as by the problem of the Logos, of speech – the problem of the reflection of desire on itself: for to philosophize is to let oneself go along with desire, but while gathering and meditating on desire, a gathering that is inseparable from speech.

Today, if anyone asks us, 'Why philosophize?', we will always be able to reply by asking the question, 'But why desire? Why is there everywhere the movement of the same seeking the other?' And we will always be able to say, until something better comes along, 'We philosophize because it [*ça*] desires.'

2

Philosophy and origin

In a youthful work, *The Difference Between Fichte's and Schelling's System of Philosophy* (1801), Hegel writes: 'When the might of union vanishes from the life of men and the antitheses lose their living connection and reciprocity and gain independence, the need of philosophy arises.'[1]

Here is a perfectly limpid reply to our question 'Why philosophize?' There is a need to philosophize because unity has been lost. The origin of philosophy is the loss of the one, the death of meaning. But *why* has unity been lost? Why have

---

1 G. W. F. Hegel, *The difference between Fichte's and Schelling's system of philosophy*, trans. H. S. Harris and Walter Cerf (Albany, NY: State University of New York Press, 1977), p. 91.

opposites become autonomous? How does it come about that mankind, which lived in unity, for which the world and mankind itself had a sense, were important, as Hegel says in the same passage, could have lost that meaning? What has happened? Where, when, how, why?

Today, we shall be examining this question of the origin of philosophy from two different points of view. First, we shall be placing ourselves on the verge of philosophy, at its origin, and trying to grasp, from the living words of one of the greatest Greek thinkers, Heraclitus, the tragic moment par excellence in which the unity of meaning is still attested, is still present to the lives of men – and the moment at which it simultaneously withdraws, conceals itself. And then, reflecting on the fact that philosophy has a history, we will proceed to a critique of this very idea of an origin, so as to show that the reason for philosophizing is permanent and always contemporary.

To begin with, let's pick up on Hegel's words, so as to understand them better; they clearly state that philosophy is born at the same time that something is dying. This something is the power of unifying. What this power unified was oppositions that, under this power, were in a living relationship and interaction. When this power withers away, the life of relationship and interaction declines and what had been united becomes autonomous, in other words no longer takes its law, its position, from anything but itself. Where there reigned a single law governing opposites, there now predominates a multiplicity of separate orders, different orders, a disorder. Philosophy is born from the mourning for unity, in separation and incoherence, rather in the same way that Claudel's *The Satin Slipper* begins. In the same work, Hegel writes, 'Dichotomy [splitting asunder, duplication, *Entzweiung*] is the source of the need of philosophy' (p. 89).

Now, what unity and what power of unification is Hegel talking about? Or – and it boils down to the same thing – what are the contraries, the oppositions whose dichotomy, whose duplication coincides with the coming of philosophy? Here is what Hegel says in the same passage: 'Antitheses such as spirit and matter, soul and body, faith and intellect, freedom and necessity, etc. used to be important; and in more limited spheres they appeared in a variety of other guises. The whole weight of human interests hung upon them' (p. 90). Let's stop here for a minute and go over this list.

The oppositions that used to be important were so significant that 'the whole weight of human interests hung upon them', says Hegel. What do these interests mean, how do they weigh on oppositions? This means that what is of interest to human beings, in other words what is between them, linking them to one another and at the same time linking their life to itself, that – this interest – used to weigh down with all its weight on these oppositions, was suspended from them, and so depended on them. An interest, in other words a relationship, which hangs upon contraries, on what is opposed – this interest turns these contraries into a couple. In the couple, there is the unity of separation and conjunction. This unity is living, since it constantly needs to create itself *in spite of* the terms it unites, since those terms thwart one another, and to create itself *in accordance with their will*, since they are its elements, they are what composes it. The couple, in the current sense of a unity of these two contraries, man and woman, probably comprises one immediate example of these contraries, an example of one of those 'other guises' whose oppositions can be meaningful 'in more limited spheres', as Hegel says. The adult and the child are of the same interest, as are day and night, winter and summer, sun and rain, life and death: these are all 'limited spheres' on which human interest indeed hangs, so many couples the alternating of whose terms provide life with its scansion, just as 'the fundamental iambus or relation between a flat and a sharp', as Claudel puts it, gives rhythm to the life of words and things.

But the contraries named by Hegel are not these ones, they are 'spirit and matter, soul and body, etc.', they are not immediate, they do not belong to limited spheres. We recognize them: these meaningful oppositions are philosophical, they are reflective (*réfléchies*). The couple formed by faith and understanding, for example, is the speculative expression of human interest in Christianity, from Saint Augustine to Saint Thomas, and perhaps up to Kant by way of Saint Anselm, it conjoins and tears apart Christian thinking and Christian life between what is given, what falls within the realm of love, and what can be conquered within the order of reason – between mystery and enlightenment.

But if these expressions of the opposition

between terms are already philosophical, does this mean that we are already in separation, in mourning for the unity of contraries? How can the two theses then go together – the thesis that philosophy is born with such a separation, and the thesis that the power of unification still governs oppositions that philosophy takes as themes?

Let's hear Hegel's words through to the end, and, as you will agree, he is here saying two apparently incompatible things. Discussing the antitheses that used to be important, such as spirit and matter, he notes: 'With the progress of culture they have passed over into such forms as the antithesis of Reason and sensibility, intelligence and nature and, with respect to the universal concept, of absolute subjectivity and absolute objectivity' (p. 90). So do we need to distinguish between a philosophy *of* and *in* life, and a philosophy *of* and *in* separation, as has been said? Or should we understand, rather, that the dichotomy from which the need for philosophy is born does not merely entail the setting aside of the two terms that results, but that this dichotomy maintains within itself, in a new form, the unity that it breaks? This is a puzzle.

PHILOSOPHY AND ORIGIN

Perhaps we will in spite of everything find an answer if we place ourselves on the verge of philosophy, to hear how it stands, in the earliest Western thinking, with the question of the one and the many, the question of the unity of contraries. Heidegger likes to say that the West is the country where the sun sets, the land of evening. When the sun sinks, men go to sleep, the world is scattered: to sleep is to withdraw from things, from men and from oneself into a world apart, into the most private life. So 'Heraclitus says that the universe for those who are awake is single and common, while in sleep each person turns aside into a private universe.'[1] Greek thought, being a Western thought, is already entering evening; but it is also the morning of thought, its awakening. So let's listen to Heraclitus, Heraclitus of Ephesus in Ionia, who expressed his views at the beginning of the fifth century BC: we shall hear his words vibrate with the most energetic affirmation that the one is there, in the many, that what we seek afar is right next to us, that the meaning

---

1 *The first philosophers: The Presocratics and the Sophists*, trans. Robin Waterfield (Oxford: Oxford University Press, 2000), p. 38 (T1).

PHILOSOPHY AND ORIGIN

of the world is nowhere other than in the world; but we shall also discern the falling of night, the threat of death, the dichotomy of meaning and reality.

To begin with, here are two fragments in which the oppositions, as Hegel says, demonstrate their unity:

> What goes against the grain is what confers, and of differences is the finest harmony.[1]

> Conjoined is what is totality and what is not totality, concordant-discordant, consonant-dissonant, and of all things one, and of one thing, all.[2]

In other fragments, the originary force of unity is manifested in its full splendour, while the very object of philosophical thought, the [sophon], is revealed as a tarrying with this force:

---

[1] This fragment is not found in Waterfield, but corresponds to B8 in Diels-Kranz: I have translated the French version given by Lyotard.

[2] This fragment is not in Waterfield, but corresponds to a fragment found in Kirk and Raven: I have again translated Lyotard's French version.

PHILOSOPHY AND ORIGIN

> It is wise (σοφόν) for those who listen not to me but to the principle (λόγος) to agree in principle (ὁμολογεῖν) that everything is one.[1]

> It is also law to follow the plan of the one.[2]

> The one wise thing (σοφόν) is to know, in sound judgement, how everything is guided in every case.[3]

But at the same time, this same unity that governs what is diverse and which it is wise (σοφόν) to know, is in other fragments called by a name that merits examination:

> It is necessary to realize that war is common, and strife is justice, and that everything happens in accordance with strife and necessity.[4]

> War is father and king of all. Some he reveals as gods, others as men; some he makes slaves, others free.[5]

---

1 *The first philosophers*, p. 39 (F10).
2 Ibid., p. 45 (F54).
3 Ibid., p. 38 (F3).
4 Ibid., p. 40 (F22), Lyotard uses the word 'debt', not 'necessity'.
5 Ibid., p. 40 (F23).

PHILOSOPHY AND ORIGIN

The one is also called war, what unites is also called what divides. It is perhaps as a result of this opposition lying at the heart of what governs all things that Heraclitus says, 'The one and only wise thing is and is not willing to be called by the name of Zeus.'[1] But it is definitely because the conjunction of the one which unites, harmony, and the one which divides, war, has everywhere a force of law that Heraclitus says, 'Harmony: non-apparent is better than apparent.'[2] But it is in another fragment in particular that we will grasp the Ephesian's full message: 'The lord whose oracle is in Delphi neither speaks nor suppresses, but indicates (σημαίνει).'[3]

I think that what we have here is the core of Heraclitus' thought, since this governor, this master, is the god, the knowledge that rules all things by running through them and making them fight each other, it is the one and it is war; and we realize that, on the one hand, this master does not speak clearly, cannot put his cards on the table so as to allow us to read him openly:

[1] Ibid., p. 38 (F4).
[2] Ibid., p. 40 (F24).
[3] Ibid., p. 40 (F26): the Greek word also means 'signifies' or 'makes a sign'.

rather, he is nothing other than the things that he governs, he is simply their arrangement, their harmony; let's say, if you like, that he doesn't *have* any game going for him, but that he *is* the order in which the values, the suits of the cards – in other words, all that exists – follow on from and contrast with each other. Or, indeed, he is the code itself, endowing the game with its rules and organizing the succession of moves into a meaningful history, and this code is nowhere but in the things that it structures and makes meaningful, without itself being a thing. And we also realize that, from another point of view, the master who has his oracle at Delphi – Apollo, the sun – does not *hide*, in other words does not hide his game, we realize that he is not trying to deceive us, to send us down a false trail, which is just what an opponent would do in a game: he is not a player, but he is the code that regulates the game and in accordance with which the players act. This code does not *hide itself*, God does not veil himself behind a curtain of clouds, he does not play hide and seek with us, he does not 'turn his face from our sight' as Saint Anselm believed (*Proslogion* 9) and as Christianity believes, he has not expelled us from his dwelling (and why indeed?), he is there as much as a code *can* be there: he is there – and this is precisely what Heraclitus says – as signifier, as what makes a sign, in other words as what, of things, makes signs.

We cannot here advance any further in the direction indicated by Heraclitus. Let's return to our question: in what sense is this thought a thought of dawn or dusk? In what way does philosophy announce itself in it, if, with Hegel, we understand by philosophy that which is needed when the oppositions lose their life, when we enter dichotomy, sundering?

We can already find some guidance on this subject in another of Heraclitus' fragments already quoted: 'Harmony: non-apparent is better than apparent.'[1] But even more, the philosopher declares with a sort of redoubled disenchantment: 'I have heard a lot of people speak, but not one has reached the point of realizing that the wise (σοφόν) is different from everything else.'[2] This 'different from everything else' sounds odd in the midst of constant emphases on the presence of the one in the many, of the profound

---

1 Ibid., p. 40 (F24).
2 Ibid., p. 39 (F11).

harmony of war and harmony. How can the λόγος that is the one be different from everything else, since everything is one? This separated unity is, so to speak, a lost unity, since it is apart from what it unites. And in our fragment, this nostalgia resulting from separation is made worse by an additional disenchantment: nobody manages to know this, to experience this retreat of the σοφόν. For – as another fragment tells us – although *logos*, i.e. meaning, is common, most people live as if they had their own way of thinking. These are probably the same people who can neither listen nor speak, and of whom Heraclitus says, 'Donkeys would prefer refuse to gold.'[1] You can see that tensions are rising; the sober serenity of 'Everything is one' is complicated by bitterness and invective, and already, like any old philosopher, Heraclitus is pointing an accusing finger at the fantasy of individual thought and the alibis of dubious values.

These things are all signs. Signs that *the* thought of Heraclitus, the theme that unity is in multiplicity both as its harmony and its contradiction at the same time – this thought is not shared,

1 Ibid., p. 39 (F17).

is not common, but is itself opposed to other thoughts and evaluations.

This means we can now understand these fragments a little better: on the one hand, they say that we should not seek unity, god, anywhere other than in diversity, since unity is the rule, the code, of this diversity; they speak of dialectics, in other words the overcoming of dichotomies, the realization that the unity of a triangle is not in the mind (of a god or a mathematician), but in the relationship between the three lines whose intersection, two by two, forges that triangle, and that the unity of the world is not in another world (the intelligible world, for example), nor in an intellect that brings its different parts together, but in the disposition and the composition (i.e. the structure) of its elements – just as a musical phrase finds its unity in the assembling, in the chain, of oppositions of value and duration between the notes composing it.

But, on the other hand, these fragments say that this harmony, which is at the same time the polemic of the elements between themselves, is neither heard nor uttered any more, that human beings are already dreaming – in other words, that they have withdrawn into the shelter of their separate worlds, and that, finally, if there is a need to attest to unity, as Heraclitus does, this is precisely because this unity is losing its witnesses, in other words, is losing itself.

And then the question already raised returns to our lips: why has there been this loss of unity and why have the contraries become autonomous? What happened? When? How? Why?

These questions cut deep. But we probably should not let ourselves be intimidated by their cutting edge. If it were true that meaning, the λόγος, the one, had been absolutely lost, one day in the past, then we would not even still know that there is a possible unity, that there has been unity, its loss itself would be lost, its death would be dead, just as a dead person ceases to be dead and really passes over when no offering shows where his tomb is, when his image is no longer maintained in any one's thought or life; then his disappearance itself disappears, he has never existed. Well, if the unity of which Hegel and Heraclitus both speak were something that had died as completely as that, we would not be able to sense their lack, our desire for them, today, and we would not be able to speak of them.

Therefore, the cutting-edge form of our

PHILOSOPHY AND ORIGIN

question 'Why has meaning been lost, why has unity been lost?' immediately blunts itself on a highly resistant material. This material is time, which preserves what it loses. The question raised invites us to answer it as historians, or at any case to seek a reply as historians; for example, to examine the evidence for what might have happened in Greece at the time of the gestation that gave birth to philosophy. And it is quite certain that we have a great deal to learn from such an investigation: not only because we still do not really know the origin of philosophy (its origin in the historical sense, in the sense in which the historian speaks of origins, sometimes even the origins of the French Revolution or the First World War), and this investigation may teach us about it, but also because we cannot for a moment cast doubt on the fact that this particular activity of philosophizing is in the same boat as, and shares the same lot as, all other activities. In other words, it bears the imprint of its time and its culture, it expresses and defines them at one and the same time – it is, just like architecture, town planning, politics or music, a necessary part *of* that whole, and necessary *to* that whole, known as the Greek world.

PHILOSOPHY AND ORIGIN

Nonetheless, by raising the question in this cutting-edge historian's way, we risk chipping its very edge. We need to understand that with the question 'why philosophize?' we are not setting out to solve a problem of origins; and there are two reasons for this:

– first of all, what concerns us is less the birth of philosophy than the death of something, a death that has a close link with this birth. It is perhaps easy, as a historian, to put a date to the birth of philosophy, for example by taking as its origin the moment when the first words of the most ancient philosopher known to us can be found (which presupposes that we already know what we are saying when we are talking about 'philosophy'). But the historian will certainly find it more difficult to define the death of what we call meaning or unity, to tie down what needs to be called meaning or unity; he will find it much more difficult to fix the time when in a certain society, the Greek society of the city states of Ionia for example, the institutions that ruled the relations between man and the world came closer or drew further away sufficiently, or at least changed in apparent size sufficiently, and fast enough, to be noticed, for them to be reflected on, for the question of their meaning to be raised, for people to start wondering why they do what they do. No Bastille fell, no head was chopped off, which would allow us to say: that was the day on which meaning was lost; and the first great loss that the historian can chalk up as one of Greece's liabilities was not the loss of unity or meaning, but the loss of Socrates, which demonstrated something quite different – that Athens did not wish, or was unable, to hear the voice through which the lack of meaning is expressed and starts to attack men and things;

– but especially, and this is the second reason, when we ask ourselves 'Why philosophize?' we are not investigating a problem of origin in the historical sense of the word: the fact that this is true is guaranteed by philosophy itself merely by dint of having or being a history. And this brings us back to the theme of time.

There is a history of philosophy, a history of desire for the σοφόν, for the One, as Heraclitus says. This history certainly means that there is a discontinuous succession of thoughts or words seeking unity: from Descartes to Kant, the words change, and thus the meanings too, the thought that circulates through the words and holds them together. A philosopher isn't someone who comes into an inheritance and starts to make it bear fruit. But his predecessors' way of asking and answering questions, a way in which he has been brought up, 'cultivated', as they say, is something that he probes, that he questions. As I've said, each time we start all over again from scratch, since each time we've lost the object of our desire. The message that comes to us from Plato's writings, for example, is one that we need to pick up, decode and recode, make unrecognizable, so as finally to be able to recognize in it, perhaps, the same desire for unity that we ourselves feel. To put it another way, the sole fact that philosophy has a history, or rather *is* history, itself has a philosophical meaning since the breaks, the cuts that segment and give rhythm to philosophical reflection and spread it across time (just like a history or story (*histoire*) – these breakages prove precisely that meaning escapes us, that the philosopher's effort to gather the dust of meaning in the hollow of meaningful words always needs to be started all over again. Husserl said that the philosopher is an eternal beginner.

However, this discontinuity points, paradoxically, to a continuity. The work of letting go and picking up again that is effected from one philosopher to another philosopher means at least that both philosophers are driven by the same desire, by the same lack. When we inspect a philosophy, I mean a set of words that forms a system, or, at least, has a meaning, this is not just in order to discover its Achilles' heel, the badly fitting or badly turned peg (or heel – *cheville*) on which we need merely to strike in order for the whole edifice to collapse; even when the philosopher criticizes the concept of the Intelligible in Plato, for example, and concludes that it's unintelligible, this isn't because he is impelled to do so by some death drive, some uncontrollable instinct pushing him on to destroy differences and reinforce the jamming that makes communication between Plato and us difficult, drowning out his message in the 'sound and fury' of 'a tale told by an idiot'.

No, it's actually quite the opposite that would happen if the death drive (as you know, this is an expression that appears in Freud's work) really did govern relations between philosophers. Freud explains that this impulse towards nothingness finds expression and rhythm in *repetition*. The person who really kills Plato, kills the contents of his words, is the person who identifies with Plato, who wants to be Plato, who seeks to repeat him.

But philosophical critique brings out the non-consistency of the system, its inconsistency (in the strong sense of the word – its insubstantiality), in order to unveil a tighter consistency, subtler and stronger, and a greater relevance to the question of the One. For all that, there is more than one philosopher – Plato, to begin with, or Kant, or Husserl – who in the course of his life performs this critique, turns round on what he has thought, undoes it and starts all over again, thus proving that the true unity of his work resides in the desire that stems from the loss of unity, and not a complacent acceptance of the fully formed system, the unity regained. What is true of one philosopher is true of the complete series of philosophers; the discontinuity that is the rule in the history that philosophy unfolds, the multi-coloured shimmer of the languages spoken in it, the muddled interception of its arguments can all have for us the value – so irritating, so disappointing – of actes manqués, of misunderstandings, of mistakes, of disorder in short, *only* because all the words spoken in them attest to a common, shared desire; and even as we deplore or mock the philosophical Tower of Babel, we are also nursing, even now, the hope for an absolute language, we are awaiting unity.

So this unity is not completely lost. The fact that there is a history of philosophy, in other words a dispersion, a discontinuity that is an essential part of the words that seek to utter this unity, does indeed show that we are not in possession of meaning; but the fact that philosophy is history, that the exchange of reasons and passions, of arguments, between philosophers, unfolds in a vast sequence that is not just random, within which something happens, rather as in a game of cards or chess – well, this proves that the segments that the diversity of individuals, cultures, epochs and classes cuts out from the fabric of the philosophical dialogue nonetheless all hang together, that there is a continuity, which is that of the desire for unity. The dichotomy of which Hegel speaks is not over, but it is in the permanent, absolute contemporaneity of this dichotomy in the continual loss of unity that philosophy can be diversified, discontinued. The separation of yesterday is the separation of today, and it's because yesterday and today are not separated that separation can be their single theme. The desire for unity attests to the absent unity, but there is the unity of desire, which bears witness to its presence.

We had asked ourselves, 'Why and how was unity lost?' This enquiry arose from the question, 'Why desire?' This in turn derived from our problem, 'Why philosophize?' Perhaps we can now start to understand that the question of the loss of unity is not merely historical, is not a question to which the historian could give a complete answer, under the heading 'The origins of philosophy'. We have just seen that history itself, and in particular the history of philosophy (but the same is true of all history), reveals in its texture that the loss of unity, the dichotomy that sets reality and meaning apart, is not an *event* in this history but, so to speak, its *motive*: specialists in criminal law use the word 'motive' to mean that which drives people to act, to kill or to steal; the loss of unity is the motive of philosophy in the sense that it is what drives us to philosophize; with the loss of unity, desire is made reflective. But musicologists also call 'motive' the phrase of a song that dominates the whole piece, giving it its melodic unity; the loss of unity thus dominates the whole history of philosophy, and turns it into a story or history.

PHILOSOPHY AND ORIGIN

As a result, if we tried to point to the seventh or fifth century BC as the historical marker of some 'origin of philosophy', we would simply be exposing ourselves to the ridicule that befalls all genetic explanation. Genetic explanation thinks it can explain the son by the father, what comes later by what comes earlier; but it forgets, suggesting its futility, that while it's true that the son results from the father – since there is no son without a father – the father's paternity depends on the son's existence, and there is no father if there is no son; all genealogy seeks to be read back to front (this is how we finally realized that the creature is the author of his author, that man made the Good Lord, as much as the other way round). The origin of philosophy is today.

One last remark: in saying this, we have no intention of wiping away history and pretending that there haven't been twenty-five centuries at least of words, and reflective words at that – of desire reflecting itself in words. My meaning is the complete opposite: giving this history its real power and its presence, its 'might of union' (Hegel), taking it seriously, means understanding that its motive, the question of unity, is forever at work within it. For if there is a history (as we said last week), this is because the conjunction of human beings with themselves and with the world is not given irreversibly, it is because the unity of the world for the mind and the unity of society for itself, and the unity of these two unities, need to be re-established all the time; history is the trace that this quest leaves behind, and the expectations it opens up ahead of itself. But these two dimensions, that of the past and that of the future, can reach out to each other from either side of the present only because this present is not full, because in its perpetual contemporaneity it conceals an absence, because it does not have unity with itself. Proust said that love is time (and also space) made perceptible to the heart; what unfolds the fan of history is the unity of the lack of unity. You will have seen that this is how philosophy is history, but not fortuitously, as an add-on, but in its very constitution, in the sense that both philosophy and history are in quest of meaning.

We know why there is a need to philosophize: it is because unity has been lost, and that we live and think in dichotomies, as Hegel says; we also know that this loss is contemporary, present, not itself lost, and that there is no trans-temporal unity, so to speak, of this loss. We'll need to ask ourselves what philosophizing has to do with this loss that is continually losing itself, this unique, permanent loss of meaning, of unity. We will examine this question next time.

3

On philosophical speech

The word 'desire', which was the object of our first reflections, comes from the Latin *de-siderare*, which means first and foremost to note with regret that the constellations, the *sidera*, do not form a sign, that the gods are not sending any messages in the stars. Desire is the disappointment of the augur. Insofar as it belongs to desire, and is perhaps the element of poverty in it, philosophy, as we have seen, begins when the gods fall silent. Nonetheless, all philosophical activity consists in speech (*la parole*). But how, then, is meaningful speech possible, if there is no sign that indicates the meaning to be uttered? What can we still say if the silence is absolute and outside us? If man is deemed to be not simply 'the measure [μέτρον] of all things', as Protagoras thought – which still implied, all the same, that these things have their own dimension, outside of man, and govern the act of measuring – but if man, in his speech, takes himself to be the source and foundation of all meaning, as it is fashionable for a certain humanism to say, whether existentialist or 'Marxist', but at any rate futile, then, as Dmitri Karamazov said, 'everything is permitted', there is no longer anything either true or false, we can say, and indeed do, anything at all, everything is absurd, or a matter of indifference.

I'd like us to examine today the relationship between philosophy and speech, focusing in particular on the character of this relationship. It is from the point of view of this contradiction that we will, I think, be able to assess philosophy's special position in speech, and the need there is for such a position. As you know, on the one hand, if nothing speaks – rather as Camus tries to show how, in *L'Étranger*, nothing speaks to Meursault, he is indifferent to everything – if nothing is already speaking when the philosopher starts to speak, then his speech is not a reply, it does not latch onto anything meaningful that is already there, it does not pursue a dialogue that has already been struck up: his speech sends its words out into the dark of night, it rambles, it makes a noise; so why, in that case, philosophize? But if, on the other hand, everything already speaks, if colours, perfumes and sounds already reply to one another, if a mathematical language arranges atoms, planets and chromosomes into a coherent discourse, if the history of human beings or of a single person is like the unfolding of an already written tale, if even the myths that people our dreams are formulated in a sort of vocabulary and articulated in a sort of syntax that constitutes the unconscious, then the same question arises: why philosophize? What more, what else can we say than what is already said? There is nothing to be added, and this time philosophical discourse is no longer an absolute noise, but the chattering of a parrot.

To begin with, let's try to get clear about certain aspects of speech, and to rid ourselves of a few pseudo-philosophical prejudices.

First, there is this current idea that we think first and then express what we think, and that this is what 'speaking' means: expressing. Thought is conceived as an internal, hidden substance, of which speech is merely the servant and the messenger delegated to deal with foreign affairs.

ON PHILOSOPHICAL SPEECH

We need to rid ourselves completely of this conception that makes thought into a thing, a *res*; we need to reject this reifying conception. For our purposes, we need to realize that to think is already to speak. We are still not thinking if we cannot name what we are thinking. And we are still not thinking if we cannot articulate and bring together what we have named. The everyday experience of finding that we lack the words to say what we want to say does not at all mean that our thought is already there, armed to the teeth, and that the words to transmit it outside have failed to turn up. When we cannot find our words, this is not because these words are failing our thought, but rather our thought that is failing to respond to what is beckoning to it.

This first remark leads us to revise two other preconceptions, the first of which is that the subject who speaks is the author of what he says. You will perhaps remember Heraclitus' fragment quoted previously: 'It is wise (σοφόν) for those who listen not to me but to the principle (λόγος) to agree in principle that everything is one.'[1] This fragment already indicated that the real subject

---

1 *The first philosophers*, p. 39 (F10).

ON PHILOSOPHICAL SPEECH

of a statement is not 'the sayer but the said'. The word 'subject' in any case attests to this double meaning: it does not refer to the person speaking, but rather the thing he is speaking about. And popular language also waxes ironical about anyone who listens to himself talking: real speech is not listening out for itself, but it seeks to let itself be guided by what it wants to say. We could spend forever here summoning all the witnesses to the trial of subjectivity. If you don't mind, let's simply quote the reflexions of John Keats in a letter (27 October 1818) to Woodhouse:

> As to the poetical Character itself [. . .] it is not itself – it has no self – it is every thing and nothing – It has no character – it enjoys light and shade; it lives in gusto, be it foul or fair, high or low, rich or poor, mean or elevated [. . .]. A Poet is the most unpoetical of any thing in existence; because he has no Identity – he is continually in for – and filling some other Body – The Sun, the Moon, the Sea and Men and Women who are creatures of impulse are poetical and have about them an unchangeable attribute – the poet has none; no identity – he is certainly the most unpoetical of all God's Creatures.

However, Keats' words risk authorizing another fantasy no less common that that of the Self: the fantasy of the Muse. According to this, the meaning within things dictates, and we have merely to transcribe; speech is already spoken even before we say it. We simply need to listen to the world, and to man, to hear speech saying what it has to say. This at least would be the case of those who are most gifted in language, the 'inspired', the 'enthusiasts' as Plato says in the *Ion*.

But things aren't so simple, and we haven't finished with speech by just putting it everywhere. When we are faced with the task of speaking, telling a story, describing a site or a face, demonstrating the properties of a geometrical figure, it's not enough for us just to lend an ear. For it isn't true that the world, things, men or combinations in space speak clearly. There is most certainly a meaning that exists ahead of our words, pulling them towards it, but until the military front of the words – so to speak – has contacted it, until this meaning has found shelter in their cohort, it will remain muddled, inaudible, as if inexistent. Consequently, if it is true that we need to hear this meaning in order to say it, the fact remains that we need to have said it for it to be heard and understood. In speaking, we are always operating on two levels at once, the level of the signifier (the words) and the level of the signified (the meaning), we are in the midst of signs, they envelope us, halt us or pull us along, they 'come' or do not come, and we try to order them from the interior, to arrange them so they will form a meaning; and at the same time we are at the side of meaning, helping it to dig out a shelter in our words, to stop it running off and escaping. Speaking is this coming and going, this *co-naissance*[1] of discourse and meaning, and it is a fantasy ever to expect that what we wish to say will reach us endowed with its freight of articulated signs, all enveloped in words. Otherwise, what we have is ready-made language, the dead letter, as in 'Hello, how are you doing?' that speaks in order to say nothing.

And if this is indeed the case, if we have to work together on language and meaning so that they will adapt to one another, as a seamstress says that a material adapts itself to her work or a sailor says that his boat adapts to the wind, this is

---

[1] '*Co-naissance*' is co-birth (i.e. a birth in which subject and object are born together) and *connaissance* (knowledge by acquaintance).

because articulate speech places the meaning that it grasps within a more differentiated symbolic system, a more 'improbable' one as information theorists call it, than the systems in which meaning was dwelling in silence and into which speech goes to seek it. Meaning is modified by the fact that it is said, and this is why saying something, naming it, means creating it, not from nothing, but setting it up in a new order, the order of discourse. There are countless examples of this: glances, smiles, asides, and silences have all woven something between a man and a woman, a certain complicity; but when this relationship is eventually declared, by one or other of them, or declares itself, then it changes, simply because it is now designated to both of them, has been given a right to speech – even if either of the two people rejects what is said. On another level: between the soldiers of the *Battleship Potemkin*, subjected to all sorts of humiliation, there are the glances, the clenched fists, the gestures that start to weave a rebellious plot; but what transforms discontent into mutiny, revolt into revolution, is – here too – speech, which points to this still nocturnal meaning, and flings it onto the bright sunlight of the beach in front of the ship after extracting it from its gangways, which takes up the latent meaning in a spontaneous movement and opens it up to further developments.

As you can see, speech changes what it utters, and this enables us to understand the apparently enigmatic *co-naissance* of signs and meaning. For it is true that the situation of being in love and the revolutionary situation do not pre-exist as such the words that designate them as loving or revolutionary, and in both cases the person who starts to speak and says 'this is what is happening', is at the same time the person who seems to be creating what he is saying, to be its author, and it is established that it is this person who, in love's tribunal or when faced with counter-revolutionary repression, takes responsibility for the situation as if he had created it and pays for the words that he has uttered – because these words are more than words. But it is also true that his speech will have an impact only if it captures something that was already there before being uttered: otherwise, it would have fallen flat.

To think, in other words to speak, lies perhaps completely in this uncomfortable situation of needing to lend an ear to a whispered meaning so as not to travesty it and having the major task of converting it into an articulate discourse if we do not want it to go astray.

I think we will have made progress in our understanding of what thinking is (and philosophy, too) when have boldly resolved to put 'theories' behind us – the theory of mind, or consciousness, or reason, and so on. For if thinking can be true, this is because there is no thinking substance, or faculty, or function, independent of what it thinks. Rather, it is insofar as it is to the thing being thought – itself, in person, as Husserl said – that speech is given. However, if this correction has the great advantage that it rids us of the aporias and the impasses that dualism and subjectivism put in the way of an understanding of thought, and spares us the monotonous, interminable arguments over the priority of mind over matter, of the subject over the object (or vice versa), it still raises other difficulties. The main one is the following:

How can things be spoken, how can articulated language gather in the meaning that floats around things, gestures, faces and situations? What pre-established harmony reigns between speech and what it says, enabling its object to receive its identity from them?

ON PHILOSOPHICAL SPEECH

I'd like to emphasize another aspect of language that we certainly need to get clear about. We do not speak alone; and even when we speak alone, we're not alone.

To speak is to communicate. But this expression in itself already potentially brings a new prejudice in its wake, or rather another manifestation of the same prejudice we have already criticized: communication, in this view, is the operation that ensures the transmission of an already prepared message to one of the poles of the system. To express is then a matter of putting something outside that had been inside – the way we shake out carpets in the fresh air. As you know, this is far from the case. Our experience of a living speech is not that of the recitation of some prefabricated discourse. It is the experience of focusing on the interlocutor, on the questions he is directing at us and the questions he forces us to direct at what we thought, at our own message, or what we thought was our message. Our experience is the experience of a game, in other words an exchange, a circulation of signs; and if this exchange is not to stumble against pure and simple repetition, against the petrification of the interlocutors in their respective positions, communication also implies the exchange of roles, implies that I am not just myself with my reasons and my passions, but also the other with *his*, and further implies that the other is also me, and thus that the other is the other of himself. In this way, we can together make a speech and, as Heraclitus would have said, we make its harmony, its unity, with the very war we wage against one another.

It will never be possible to understand that communication is possible if we begin by enclosing each message, the other's as well as ours, in our respective subjectivities. We would then find ourselves faced by a problem rather similar to the one we have just mentioned (the problem of how silent meaning gains access to meaningful speech): we would need to solve the riddle of a pure interiority, our own. But to speak, which is to think, is immediately communication, in other words bears within it the ability to be on the other side of myself, outside, so to speak (but where is the inside?); and it has become common to observe, with child psychologists, that learning language happens at the same time as learning about ubiquity: the child begins to use the persons and tenses of grammar, and thus really to articulate the meaning he is uttering, at the very same time that he shows himself able, in a game, or in the real family configuration, to exchange his role with his father's role, for example, or his younger brother's, or his mother's.

When we enter the order of language that is also the order of thought, we enter the order of sociability. For we take possession of a system – or we are taken over by a system – of phonetic signs, the language of our culture, thanks to which not only can silent meaning be articulated in a discourse, but thanks to which, too, what we have to say immediately finds the path leading to others by virtue of the fact that this as yet inarticulate meaning cuts its words out of a network of signs to which the other and myself together belong.

This – very quick – detour through an investigation of speech will perhaps help us now understand a little more clearly what philosophical speech is, speech as language, and, since this is our problem, why there is a need for this speech.

The various paths we have just traced all lead to the same crossroads: speech comes from further and deeper than the speaker himself, and enfolds interlocutors in the same domain of signs, and is already inarticulately present to what is not yet said. Perhaps we will not find any better summary of these conclusions than in two passages from Paul Claudel's *Poetic Art*:

> A long time ago, in Japan, while going up from Nikko to Chuzenji, I saw, juxtaposed by my line of vision, although at a great distance from each other, the green of a maple tree filling the separating space, in order to answer the appeal of a pine, asking for agreement. These pages are meant to be the beginning of a text on forests, the arborescent enunciation by June, of a New Art of Poetry of the Universe, of a new Logic. The old one used syllogisms as an instrument of expression, the new one uses metaphor, the new word, the operation resulting of the sole, conjoint and simultaneous existence of two different things. The first one has a general and absolute affirmation as a starting point, the attribution, once and for all, of a quality, of a property to the subject. No matter what the time and place, *the sun shines, the sum of the angles of a triangle is equal to two right angles.* It creates abstract individuals, by defining them; it establishes invariable series between them. Its method consists in naming. All these terms, once chosen, classified according

to type and species in the columns of its repertory, after individual analysis, are applied to all subjects brought to its attention. I compare this kind of logic to the first part of grammar, which determines the nature and function of the different words. The second Logic would be more like the syntax of such a grammar, teaching the art of fitting words together and is practised before our eyes by nature itself. There is only one science, that of the general, there is no creation, but of the particular. The metaphor, the fundamental iambus or the connection between a flat and a sharp does not play only in the pages of our books: it is the autochthonous art used by all that which is born. And do not call it chance. The plantation of this bouquet of pines, the shape of this mountain are no more due to chance than the Parthenon or this diamond, in the cutting of which the lapidary grows old, but is the product of a treasure of richer and more scholarly aims. I quote various proofs of geology and climate, natural and human history; our achievements and the means we use do not differ from those of nature. I understand that no thing survives by itself, but in its infinite relationship with all others.

ON PHILOSOPHICAL SPEECH

[...]

Nothing is complete in itself; all is drawn from within by itself, from the outside by the vacuum, delineated by its absent form, as each trait is determined by the others. The lake paints on the oval sky the white swan clinging unto it, the bull's eye, the fodder and the shepherd girl. A gust of wind sweeps off, in one blow, the spittle from the sea, the leaf and the bird from the bush, the bonnet from the peasant's head, the smoke from the village and the chimes from the steeple. When dawn comes to life, the vegetable and animal kingdom come out of sleep, like a face slowly overtaken by intelligence. And some ordinary themes are offered to the reflection of various things. The whole surface of the earth and the grass that covers it and the animals that populate it is as sensitive as a plate acted upon by the photographic sun. It is a vast workshop in which everyone endeavors to *render* the color it takes from the solar hearth.

Things have two means of knowing each other, that is, in the sense adopted in this paragraph, of completing each other in space, by being either contiguous or complementary.

They all fit into a more general form, combine into a *picture*: it belongs to each point of view to look for and find the eyes *owing to which* they exist. And just as we know things by deciding upon a general characteristic we grant to them, they know each other by taking advantage of a common principle, that is, light similar to a seeing eye. Each of them complies with the necessity of being seen. The rose or the poppy sign in red the bond with the sun, according to which, other flowers are compelled to be white or blue. A certain green could not exist by itself any more than a mass without a prop. Each note of a scale calls for and implies the others. None of them aspires to satisfy the feelings all by itself. It exists on condition that it should not sound like the others, but also on the imperative condition that the others should sound as it does not. There is knowledge of each other, obligation between them, thus relationship between the various parts of the world, as between the parts of speech, so that they may constitute a readable sentence; and, similarly, there is a consistency in sentiments, as in the words expressing them; and movements follow a pattern, as proven by hours. The wheelwork manufacturing it could not stop any more than time itself.[1]

In this second passage, what is mainly emphasized and highlighted is the speaking character of the universal concert; and this happens in the following way: if the world is a language, this is because each thing in it is opposed to the others and calls upon them to take on meaning.

Now if one day you open the *Course on General Linguistics* by Ferdinand de Saussure, you'll find the following remarks:

> In language there are only differences. Even more important: a difference generally implies positive terms between which the difference is set up; but in language there are only differences *without positive terms*. Whether we take the signified or the signifier, language has neither ideas nor sounds that existed before the linguistic system, but only conceptual and phonic differences that have issued from the system. The idea

---

[1] Paul Claudel, *Poetic art*, trans. Renee Spodheim (Washington, NY; London: Kennikat Press, 1969), pp. 31–2 and pp. 47–8.

or phonic substance that a sign contains is of less importance than the other signs that surround it. [. . .]

Between them [signs] there is only *opposition.* [. . .]

In language, as in any semiological system, whatever distinguishes one sign from the others constitutes it. [. . .]

Putting it another way, *language is a form and not a substance.*[1]

Now re-open Claudel with Saussure's key: Claudel is simply saying that the whole of reality is the language spoken by God.

Now philosophizing begins at the same time that God falls silent, the time of distress, as Hölderlin said, the time when the unity of the multiplicity formed by things is lost, when the different ceases to confer, the dissonant to be

---

[1] Ferdinand de Saussure, *Course in general linguistics*, ed. Charles Bally and Albert Sechehaye with the collaboration of Albert Riedlinger; trans. and annotated by Roy Harris (London: Duckworth, 1983), pp. 120–2.

consonant, war to be harmony, as Heraclitus put it.

It is philosophy's paradox that it is a speech that arises when the world and man seem to speak no longer, a speech that *de-siderat*, desires, a speech that the silence of the stars has deprived of the speech of the gods.

Take Claudel's work, for instance, in which the poetic and religious dimensions are mixed up together: it draws its energy, its ability to become swept away, from the fact that it establishes itself in a world completely peopled by signs, and does not hesitate to decipher everywhere (even in the great sensual blaze of *Break of Noon*) a single speech, the word[1] that was in the beginning. But the philosopher is, rather, the person who starts to speak in quest of this word, and so does not possess it in the beginning, and wants to possess it at the end, and never ceases to possess it.

You'll start telling me that after all, the man of faith, the priest, isn't Claudel either, in possession of the divine semantics; he needs to venture on an interpretation of signs, and he too is free,

---

1 *Le verbe* is sometimes used in French translations of the New Testament to translate λόγος, 'the word' as in John 1:1.

in this initial sense that he does not know all the clauses of the pact that links him to God's logic – that he can, that he must err.

Indeed: but that faith is already a sick faith, and the Christian world is already a sick world, a world in which the son of God died, a culture, as you know full well, which had to make due place for philosophy, in other words the question of its meaning, seeking understanding (as Saint Anselm said). This is a religion that can incorporate into its code even erring and straying – in other words, the lack of code.

And then, on the other hand, it was also in this world that science was able to begin. Now science endeavours nothing less than to develop a language that can speak things exactly without being refuted by them. And the project of this language, whose grammar is mathematics, rests primarily on the altogether irreligious conviction that the cipher has been lost, that facts do not speak, that we need to invent a new logic and axiomatics, not so that the dialogue between mind and things can be resumed – a hope that science has never nursed – but at least so that the utterances of the scientist will find in the world the, as it were, mute respondent, the impenetrable acquiescence that a successful experiment provides. Whatever we may say about it, what irreversibly separates the sorcerer from the scientist, the shaman from the doctor, is that the former – rather like Claudel – is in the grip of the universal symbolic system, belongs to it, and his speech is effective only insofar as it is heard by the men of his culture – including himself – as the very word (*verbe*) that gives order to the universe. The scientist, on the other hand, is in the grip of nothing but the chill absence of any such symbolic system, and is fascinated instead by chance, contingency, disorder; he knows that he cannot absorb them into an order, into a network of reasons or laws, unless he himself fabricates this order on the basis of ambiguous signs; and even when, in some theory, he seems to have allowed the unity awaiting expression in the multiplicity of facts to speak, he constantly suspects this unity of being merely the echo of his own discourse. There is a disenchantment within science; the vogue for antibiotics, missiles and psychoanalysts may arouse among laymen the mixture of belief and fear that is the sign of the sacred, but it actually demonstrates the lack of that sacred.

If the scientist turns with scandalized contempt

away from his own popularity, this is precisely because he has absolutely no intention of restoring or establishing a general symbolic system of the world (a religion): he knows he is alone, and that he faces a silent world.

Philosophical speech is not the speech of either faith or science. It is not on the same level as the symbolic order, or the logic of metaphor, where everything is a sign; but neither does it accept that meaning is altogether its responsibility and that, like the scientists in his laboratory, it needs to provide both the questions and the answers.

Faced with poetics, the philosopher says – as I have just said to you about Christianity – that this speech (*parole*), so sure of being merely a spokesman (*porte-parole*), must after all invent the meaning that it reveals, or in any case find the words in which this meaning can be grasped. After all, Moses was alone on Sinai, and only God could attest that he didn't make up some of the words on the Tables of the Law. Saying this means that we put back in its place the risky element in speech, the active force with which it converts inarticulate meaning into discourse.

But on the other hand, philosophy, which is

opposed to the formalism of scientific axiomatics, remains flabbergasted at this extravagance; a language built in a vacuum, and yet still able to find under it things that allow themselves to be expressed by it; philosophy keeps chewing over Einstein's naive words, 'the most incomprehensible thing about the world is that it is comprehensible'. And philosophy then asks science whether the apparently so abstract, so detached edifice of the intuitions through which we hold onto things and they hold onto us does not, all the same, rest on an originary spiriting away of the body and the world, of the sensible (*sensible*: what we can sense) and the sensitive (*sensible*: what can sense), of silence and language – does not rest on a colloquy prior to all articulated dialogue. And this time, saying as much means restoring responsibility for speech to its proper rank, to its truth, to its passive strength that can attest to a meaning already there.

And this twofold critique, or this reflection that looks both ways, is one that the philosopher also turns on his own speech, and this is how philosophical speech is defined, and why it irritates everybody. We were saying just now that, when we speak, we are on both sides at once: on the side of meaning, and on the side of the signifier, joining them together. Philosophical speech takes this ubiquity to its extreme, to its paroxysm; it is not altogether what it says, it does not allow – or it tries not to allow – itself to be grasped by the autonomous impulse of its themes, it wants to unearth the metaphors, sift the symbols, test the articulations of its discourse, and this leads it to form as purified a language as possible, to seek a rigorous logic and axioms on which and with which a logic without any intermittence, without any lacuna, in other words without any unconscious, can be uttered. The proposition that opens the first part of the *Ethics*: 'I understand by cause of itself that whose essence involves its existence', in other words God, a proposition that screeches like a diamond scratching into glass, this proposition – like the whole oeuvre of Spinoza the grinder of lenses – has the vocation of transparency.

But at the same time, the philosophical discourse does not belong to itself, it does not possess itself, and it knows that it does not possess itself, and it hopes passionately not to possess itself. For if there were nothing more in its word (*verbe*) than what a limpid consciousness seeks to put there,

there would be nothing; philosophical language would be as empty as an auditorium before the show starts, like an axiomatics, in other words a logic of anything at all, an object in general; hence its ability to capture latent meanings, to articulate them so as to put them into circulation, to enable all other people to share them – its ability to find an echo with others because it is an echo itself, its ability to make itself heard, because it too hears – this ability would be destroyed. It would not be at all difficult to locate, in the apparently smooth path followed by Descartes's thought in the *Meditations*, the cracks, the discontinuities, the shadows that interrupt the luminous course of the seasons; there is a latent meaning, ungrasped, that slips in between the lacunae of the manifest meaning, and that simultaneously forces apart the segments that it cuts out of it and yet makes them hold together. And after all, what else does Descartes say when, once the *cogito* of the *Second Meditation* has been solidly established, he recognizes in the *Third Meditation* that this absolute point of anchorage is itself anchored in another harbour, which is God, so that when we say 'I think', we are saying that God, that 'it' (*ça*) is thinking in our thought? Today, philosophical speech knows that it can also be understood as a dream narrative, as a speech in which it speaks (*ça parle*), even though it dreams of a total rigour, dreams of being able to keep its eyes wide open. This is why the time of metaphysical systems is over.

You need to realize that you won't obtain any answer to your question from philosophy, if you ask it for everything; for the child, too, there comes a time when the mother can no longer be the answer to everything. Philosophers can give their word as much as they like, their word (*parole*) contains both more and less than what we ask of them. It contains less because the discourse they offer us remains unfinished, does not manage to close in on itself, to be self-sufficient, as, for example, a dictionary does when each word (*mot*) little by little refers to all the other words and to nothing else: but the philosopher cannot forget that this chain of signs, this kind of infinite recurrence in the shape of a circle, presupposes our initial access to language, and if we are going to manage to swim along with words, we need to be in the stream already, with all of our unsaid experience, and the philosopher knows that it is this presence of the unsaid in the act of saying that comprises its truth, prior to all definition. But philosophical speech contains more than what it thinks it is giving, precisely because it carries more sounds than it would like, because it makes underground meanings rise to the surface without designating them, and it thus merits a hearing comparable with that of the poet or the dreamer.

Philosophical speech explicitly aims at truth, but misses it; and yet only insofar as philosophy is at the side of what it says, that it speaks in an aside, is it true. We could say of its relationship with truth what Du Bellay wrote in the twelfth sonnet of his *Olive*:

> L'obscur m'est clair, et la lumière obscure;
> Vôtre je suis et ne puis être mien [. . .]
> Obtenir veux et ne puis requérir.
> Ainsi me blesse et ne me veut guérir
> Ce vieil enfant, aveugle, archer, et nu.

> The dark to me is clear, the light is dark;
> All yours I am and cannot be my own [. . .]
> To gain I want and cannot ask for gain.
> And so wounds me, and will not make me whole
> That aged child, blind, naked, with his bow.

ON PHILOSOPHICAL SPEECH

Philosophical speech does not capture desire; on the contrary, it is the aged, naked child who is the master of this speech too.

We said at the start that, with philosophy, desire is reflected. We know that this reflection, this repetition, is something that we owe to speech, more precisely to the speech that at one and the same time allows itself and does not allow itself to be mastered by what it has to say, just as Socrates accepts Alcibiades' desire, but still problematizes it. We can see that reflection, and speech even at its most concerted, does not spare the philosopher from the law of desire, the blindness and the wound of the child with the bow, the childhood through which the world holds onto us. The opposition between absence and presence and the movement that is born between the terms is something that we thus find at the very heart of language; on the one hand, it is the development of discourse in the pursuit of its full meaning, it is the poverty of meaning found in all speech and, on the other hand, it is the envelopment of speech within meaning, its excess of meaningfulness, its resource. Speech is philosophical not because it hopes to reply to the question raised by desire with words, with a system, as clear as a fantasy, but only because it knows that, like all speech, it is grasped even at the very moment that it most wants to grasp.

By reflecting itself in philosophical speech, desire recognizes itself as this *too much* meaning and this *too little* meaning, which is the law of all language.

> Today, we can reply to:
> 'Why philosophize?' by yet another question:
> 'Why speak?' and, since speak we do:
> 'What does speaking seek to say and yet cannot say?'

4

On philosophy and action

In the first of the four lectures, with the last one today, we have tried to establish that philosophy belongs to desire as much as anything *can* belong to desire; it is not different in nature from any 'simple' passion, but simply this desire, this passion that turns round upon itself, reflects itself – this desire, in short, which desires itself.

In the second lecture, we saw that trying to seek an origin for philosophy is a rather vain enterprise, since the lack from which we suffer, and that arouses philosophy – the loss of unity – is not over with, is not past and gone, but happens this time too, again and again, in other words never stops repeating itself – and that philosophy thus has its origin in itself, and is in this respect history.

In the third lecture, we examined the potential nature of philosophical speech, and we concluded in short that this speech cannot close itself up in a coherent and self-sufficient discourse (we used the example of a dictionary to prove this), but always falls short of what it wants to say, does not say enough about it – and also goes too far, says too much about it – and, finally, that philosophical speech itself knows this.

If we now gather all this up together in one fell swoop, we will be forced to conclude that philosophizing is undoubtedly of no use, and leads nowhere, since it is a discourse that never sets down its definitive conclusions, since it is a desire that indefinitely drags its desire along with it, a lack that it can never fill. The philosopher is perpetually poverty-stricken, living off language as a make-do, and he may cut a sorry figure in the eyes of his colleagues – *they*, after all, have things to teach you. What use, after all, *is* philosophy? That's the question we ask ourselves. A rumour coming down from the Tribunal of Athens, one day in 399 BC, says that, well, it's of no use at all, and this rumour cries from afar against the philosopher: to death with him.

Today, in our developed countries, philosophers

are not usually put to death, at least not by being forced to drink a big glassful of hemlock. But it is possible to kill philosophy without poisoning the philosopher. You can stop the philosopher being there, being present with his lack in society, you can stop him calling on someone responsible for religious observance, for example, and asking him innocently what piety is, as Socrates used to do. You can stop the philosopher doing that, you can send him off somewhere, send him right away, so that his absence will not make too much noise, will not make too much of a discord with the rich melody of development. In short, the philosopher will just interpret the world, which lies outside, on the doorstep: this doesn't bother anyone. Likewise, from time to time, one or two 'ideas' might emerge from this cloistered rumination, ideas that can perhaps be used if skilful and patient technicians manage to change them into tools for transforming things and especially for transforming human beings.

You will know the last, eleventh *Thesis on Feuerbach* written by the young Marx around 1845. This is what it says: 'Philosophers have merely interpreted the world in different ways; the point is to change it.' I think that, in Marx's

ON PHILOSOPHY AND ACTION

thesis here, we have a good point of departure for reflecting on the real extent of the impotence, the incompetence, the ineffectiveness of philosophy. In spite of the peremptory character of the young Marx's formula, we shall see that things are not simple, and we shall understand this not in opposition to Marx and true Marxism, but *thanks to* them; there are not those who speak on the one hand, and those who act on the other.

Last week, we said that the act of saying transforms what is said; and you also know that we cannot act without knowing what we want to do, in other words without saying it, without discussing it, with ourselves or with others. This immediately gives us two reasons to re-establish the contact between philosophy and action; but let's try to examine this reciprocal overlap between saying and doing in a little more depth.

In Marxism, there is an apparently decisive, radical critique of philosophy. And the radical character of this critique results precisely from the fact that Marx gives philosophy its full depth, takes it completely seriously, and does not simply content himself with dismissing it for its verbal incontinence. Not only does Marx show that philosophy is a reflection separate from reality, that it has a spiritual existence cut off from existence tout court, as we've just said, but he also shows that this separate reflection is unconsciously haunted by reality, by the lives and problems of real men, by the real social problematic. What Marxism calls ideology (and philosophy is in the front rank of ideology) is not simply an autonomous representation of reality, with the philosopher, the thinker in his corner, coming up with his mad ideas all by himself, so that in short mankind would cart along with it – throughout its history, without any profit but without any great loss either – those crazy chatterboxes known as philosophers. No, Marx did not hold Hegel's lesson so cheap, he did not forget that the content of a false position is not false in itself, but only if it is isolated, taken as absolute. If, rather, it is gathered together with that from which it has been separated, this content appears as a moment, an element of truth in its march.

And so even a false consciousness, even an ideology such as the most apparently sublimated (*quintessencié*) philosophical reflection, that of Plotinus or Kant if you like, has its reason in the Marxist sense; in other words, its roots plunge, as a result of its very problematic, into the reality with which its summit, its culmination seems in complete disagreement.

If, for example, from the philosophy of Descartes to Kant, freedom appears as a theme that is increasingly set at the heart of the way man and the world are conceived, as an ever more decisive concept of theory, this is because in practice a current is starting to form, is swelling into a wave that will submerge Europe with and after the French Revolution: it is because a new social and human world is gestating in the same old world that is stopping it from coming to maturity, and this new world finds a possible expression of its own desire in the philosophical problematic of freedom. Not an expression that has been prepared long since (as you know, for example, this theme of freedom is not really predominant in Greek philosophy), but rather a sort of ideological receptacle in which this current, this new world, will be able to find accommodation, to register its aspirations. And if this current is oppressed in reality, if a real desire cannot manifest itself in person, simply cannot, or in other words does not have the power, the power to organize men and things in accordance with itself, with this desire, then this current tells its story differently, disguises itself, plays the game of power in another sphere of reality. And then we have ideology, we have philosophy.

This conception, we should note in passing, is very close – as regards the situation it ascribes to what is false, what is mystified – very close to Freud's. For Freud, at least as a first approximation (and perhaps superficially), it is likewise the conflict of the libido, the instincts, with what is given by reality, in particular the child's tendency to see his mother as protection, as absolute security, as a reply to everything, versus the fact that he is forbidden to keep her for himself, to marry her, even if only in the imagination – it is this conflict that arouses those very 'ideologies' in the analytical sense, namely the fantasies produced by the dream, by neurosis or even sublimation.

At this point, the Marxist critique of philosophy shows its full profundity. Philosophy is not false in the same way as is the judgement that states that the wall is green when it is actually red.

Philosophy is false insofar as it shifts into another world, the 'metaphysical' world, sublimating, as Freud would put it, what belongs to this world and to this world alone.

So there is a truth of ideology, it echoes a

real problematic, that of its own time; but its falsity lies in how its echo to this problematic, the very way in which it forms and establishes the problems of real men, rises above the real world and does not lead to any resolution of these problems.

It could be said that this characterization of philosophy as ideology, this critique of philosophy, is a radical critique, since it implies that, in the final analysis, there is no specifically philosophical dimension, since philosophical questions are not philosophical questions, but real questions transcribed and encoded in another language that is mystified and mystifying, being other. The reality of philosophy results solely from the *unreality of reality*, so to speak; it results from the lack experienced in reality, it springs from the way that desire for something else, for another organization of the relations between human beings, a desire that is at work in society, does not manage to free itself from the old social forms. Thus it is because the human world (and for Marx this human world is at once the individual world and the inter-individual, social world), the real human world is lacking in something and there is desire in it that philosophy can build in this lack a non-human, metaphysical world, an elsewhere, a beyond.

As you can see, Marx doesn't give short shrift to philosophy, he takes it in its most profound aspect, desire, and shows clearly that it is the daughter of desire.

However, at the same time he reveals, as a result of this very same situation, the essential impotence of philosophy. Seen from Marx's angle, philosophy seeks its own end: it would like to give in speech a definitive answer to the question of this lack that lies at its origin. (Note in passing that this assessment of philosophy as the presumption of a total, self-sufficient discourse stems from Hegel's influence on Marx: Hegel said that the True is the Whole, that the Absolute is essentially Result, in other words that only at the end is it what it truly is.) For Marx, as for Hegel, philosophy seeks the death of philosophy, for such is its most authentic passion; this death would indeed mean that there is no more need to philosophize; and if there were no need to philosophize, this would be the sign that the lack that lies at the root of this need to philosophize, namely desire, has been satisfied. But the problem is precisely that philosophy understood as ideology in Marx's sense cannot bring itself to a conclusion, cannot put an end to itself, since it owes its existence solely to this lack in human reality, since it relies on its lack to try and fill it with speech, and since philosophical speech, being philosophical, in other words ideological, in other words alienated, cannot fill the real lack, since it speaks to one side, beyond, elsewhere. It is the equivalent of seeking a solution to the problems an individual encounters in reality by elaborating some harmonious dream.

The words 'the point is now to change the world' thus mean that we need to modify reality, change life, so that there is no more need to dream, I mean to philosophize, that we need to enter into possession of ourselves not through that separate and crazy world of nocturnal sleep, but in broad daylight, in this world that we all have in common, when our eyes are open and our gaze is new or naive, when we are standing erect. And what can the philosopher do when faced with this realistic demand, when he is lying down, in the darkness of some *different* place?

But now, let's turn – along with Marx himself and the whole history of the world over the past century, a history marked so deeply by Marxism, let's turn to this action in broad daylight that he proposes to us, this endeavour to 'change the world' to which – with the impatience and anger of things that cannot wait – the eleventh *Thesis on Feuerbach* summons us.

The first thing that needs to be said – it is self-evident, for a Marxist, but is still worth noting – is that practice, the action of transforming reality, is not any random activity: not every activity really transforms its object. There are false activities – those that have a superficial appearance of effectiveness, obtaining as they do an immediate result, but that do not really transform things. A politician in the current sense of the term, a leader in the current sense, who has a diary filled to bursting with meetings, who has four telephones on his desk and dictates three letters simultaneously, who with his eloquence can bring packed auditoria to their feet, who has twenty thousand people at his beck and call, isn't necessarily someone who transforms reality. He may simply be someone who maintains what is, who preserves things, preserves relations between human beings in their prior state, or rather who develops them or helps them to develop while taking care there are no bumpy rides – in other words, without accepting that this development might *really* transform what is developing (as if a mother wished her child to develop, but without allowing him ever to become an adult, on the pretext that he would then no longer be her child, a child like he was at the beginning).

Activities of this type, whether conservative or reformist, are equally far removed from any transformative action. A transformative action, in the sense that Marx's formula takes it, consists (envisaged from the point of view we adopted in tackling this problem, namely the relation with philosophy and action), consists in destroying or helping to destroy what makes false conscience, philosophy, and ideology in general possible, to fill in practical terms the lack from which ideological aberrations arise.

This being said, what does such a transformation consist of? You will realize how much, for Marx (and for us, who have the irreversible advantage over him of a century of additional practice, and of practice that was Marxist in intention), action is not a simple matter, a pure operation.

Transforming the world doesn't mean doing just anything. If the world needs to be transformed, this is because it contains within itself the aspiration to something else; what it lacks is already there, its own absence from itself is present. And it is only this that those famous words mean: 'Mankind thus inevitably sets itself only such tasks as it is able to solve.' If there were not what Marxists call 'tendencies' in reality, there would be no possible transformation, and as we were saying the other day in connection with speech, everything would be permitted, we would be able, not just to say, but to do anything at all. If the world needs to be transformed, this is because it is already transformed. There is in the present something that announces, anticipates and beckons the future. Mankind at a given moment is not simply what it seems to be, what a good psycho-social survey might be able to photograph (and that's why this kind of photographic survey is always terribly disappointing due to the poverty of the snapshots it produces), mankind is also what it is not yet, what it is seeking, confusedly, to become.

To use another terminology, the one we were using in the last lecture, let's say that there is meaning already there, hanging round in things, in the relations between human beings, and that really transforming the world means setting free this meaning, giving it its full power.

You will by now be aware of the deep analogy there is between speaking and doing. We've said that speaking gathered up and raised into articulate discourse a latent, silent meaning, 'rolled in the wave of mute communication' (as Merleau-Ponty puts it). And we said that it is this meaning, at once present and absent, which endows this transcription that is speech not only with its full responsibility, its risk of error, but also its possibility of being true.

Now it is this same problem that arises for action, in other words for the transformation of the world: what is the latent meaning of reality, what is the aspiration, what the desire, and how can it be expressed so that it may act, in other words so that it may have power?

Transformative action cannot manage without a 'theory' in the true sense of the world, in other words a speech that risks saying, 'This is what's happening, this is where it's going', and that ipso facto starts to organize, at least in discourse, this It [*ce Ça*]; it needs a speech that really desires the desire for reality, or that desires with the same desire as does reality.

'It is not enough,' Marx said, 'for thought to strive for realization, reality must itself strive towards thought' (*A contribution to the critique of Hegel's philosophy of right*). Only if reality comes to thought, if the world comes to speech, can thought and speech be true.

So we can see that action, understood as the transformation of the world (the only transformation worthy of the name) presupposes – and this is its potential guarantee – the paradoxical passivity of which Keats spoke in the letter we read the other day. We need to receive in order to give, we need to hear in order to say, we need to gather in order to transform, and it's perhaps no coincidence that the Greeks had the same word for the action of gathering and the action of saying.

So you can see that by 'throwing ourselves into action', as the saying goes, we do not evade – we evade less than ever – this necessity, this law of the debt as Heraclitus put it, which turns action as well as speech, my relation with the other and my bodily existence, into an exchange. Only the blindness proper to our time, the redoubtable falsification of the very meaning of action, mean that – as happens in our civilization – action and manipulation, action and conquest, can be confused. Marx still knew – and his official successors have completely forgotten this in reality, even if Marx's words are forever on their lips – Marx knew that doing also means allowing oneself to be done to, and this passivity requires the greatest energy.

Now that we have reached this point of our analysis, and without having left the Marxist critique of philosophy by a hair's breadth, we can raise the question of the action of transforming the world as it actually arises: how can we know that the reading we are going to give of reality is the right one; that the aspiration, the tendency on which we are going to base our transformative work is indeed the aspiration, the tendency that is really at work in the world?

After the critique of ideology, it must be clear that for Marxism there are no Tables of the Law, no revelation.

We cannot place our trust in a speech that has already been uttered elsewhere, in a law established in the beyond, coming from the depths of things (in any case, there is no such thing for anyone, as we said the other day), and this is what Marx thinks: for the Christian himself always needs to reinvent the Law that he thinks has been written since the beginning of time, he needs to rewrite it, or rather write it himself, in the choices he makes every day, in his relations with other people and himself, in what he thinks he must accept and what he thinks he must reject; Christians, and they will bear me out on this, still need to discuss, to come to an agreement, to take counsel or summon councils. As a result, the absolute transcendence of the law is not experienced as such, it is not, in the strict sense of the term, viable.

This means that in the field of history and society, in the domain of relations between human beings taken in their becoming, there is no written law that determines the meaning of history and the meaning of society; this means that we need to abandon the idea that has dominated and still dominates the philosophy of history and action, which is, indeed, a metaphysical idea – that this whole disorder of societies that develop from different positions and at different speeds, that the conflict, and the struggle between social classes – that all this leads to revolution as to its resolution, that all this winds to its end just as the river winds to the sea. We cannot argue that there is a meaning to history of which we are the holders, the owners, and thus decode the apparent disorder and display the real order, in short carry out an infallible politics. There is no infallible politics. Nothing can be taken for granted.

Allow me a short detour, which I think will shed light on things. In a book that has always had and still has a great impact on ways of thinking and acting in our period (*The human use of human beings: cybernetics and society*), the author, Norbert Wiener, writes that the true vision of the world for the scientist cannot be Manichaean but Augustinian.

This is what Wiener says:

> [. . .] the black in the world [i.e. its opacity, its unintelligibility, its disorder] is negative and is the mere absence of white [i.e. clarity, reason, etc. – this is the Augustinian conception: there is no autonomous principle of Evil, of Error], while in Manichaeanism, black and white belong to two opposed armies drawn up in line facing one another.[1]

---

[1] Norbert Wiener, *The human use of human beings: Cybernetics and society* (Boston: Houghton Mifflin, 1950), p. 190.

And it is true that the physical world, for example, does not set up a concerted opposition to the efforts we make to understand it; it does not hide its meaning deliberately so as to mislead and undo the scientist. But when it comes to society, history, politics (in other words the problem of the community of human beings), is this rejection of Manichaeism, in other words of a conception of there being an enemy opposite, playing his game against me who am his enemy, is this rejection of Manichaeism correct? Let's take up the words of the Marxist problematic again: why is it that society, which is big with meaning, which is haunted by a spectre, as the beginning of the *Communist Manifesto* puts it, which is haunted by a lack, cannot give birth to this meaning without violence? Why can it not manage to say clearly what is wrong with it, unless there is something stopping it? And if there is something stopping it, is this not because there is an army drawn up in line, an enemy facing this aspiration, deliberately and resolutely trying to repress it?

But saying this is still not enough, and Marxism is not as naively Manichaean as Wiener seems to believe. He knows perfectly well that there are not two enemies lined up facing one another like the pieces on a chessboard at the beginning of the game; he knows perfectly well that the game has been in progress for quite a while already, that the pieces are both engaged with each other and against the others, that they form a totality of relations that is at once a relation of complement and contrariety. This means that the enemy is not outside, but also within.

And we need to understand this 'within' with the greatest degree of penetration: the enemy is within thought itself.

The fracturing of society in the form of social classes is also a fracturing of practice, in other words of the silent transformation of social relations, and its separation from society.

The interpretation of reality, the understanding of the statement of what society really desires, and thus revolutionary theory itself in the eyes of Marxism itself, is normally cut off from practice, it is more or less continuously imbued by what Marx calls the dominant ideas that are, he says, the ideas of the dominant classes. The link between theory and practice is thus ceaselessly exposed to error, to mystification. As a result, for Marx, speech cannot come to meet what needs it in a simple, innocent way so to speak, but in a contradictory way. The movement towards something else that drives society, its absolute lack, which Marx saw embodied in the proletariat, in that class, he said, against which 'no *particular* wrong, but *wrong* generally' has been perpetuated, the proletariat as lack and movement cannot have access spontaneously to language and articulation, to theory and organization. Between this desire, this tacit meaning of which the proletariat consists, and this desire for desire, this explicit meaning, which it has to be in order to find an effective solution to the separation and disorder in which it is immersed, as well as the whole of society, there lies the responsibility and the risk of a speech, of a theory and an organization that is in principle (and right from the start) separated from this desire, isolated from the proletariat. This theory needs to bring itself into unison with the proletariat's lack so as to be able to reflect it.

We are still 'in the true', since the latent meaning within things, in the world around us, between us and within us, encroaches on speech, sustains and guides the meaning that is articulated in it: but we are not 'in the true', we are not there because a gap keeps reality as a whole beyond what we can say of it, beyond our 'consciousness'. To think, from the point of view of action (but it's true in any case), does not mean to enter into something already thought, to enter into an articulation already established; it means, first and foremost, to struggle against all that separates (today, in the time when we exist) the signified from the signifier, against all that prevents desire from starting to speak and through its speech gaining power.

As you can see, Marxism is very far removed from Manichaeism. Theory (beginning with Marxism itself) is continually undermined by its social and historical position as ideology, it is continually threatened, not by betrayals, as the Manichaeans say, but from within, by a fall into what has already been thought, by degenerating into what has already become established. Capitalism is not a 'camp', as is said these days, it is the opacity that slips between human beings and what they do, between human beings and others, and also between human beings and what they think; and it would be easy to detect this capitalism – as reification, as Lukács put it – right in the middle of established Marxism, within the supposedly revolutionary good conscience.

We were asking ourselves: but what is the

point of philosophy, since philosophy, by its own avowal, cannot produce results, cannot conclude any system, and, strictly speaking, leads nowhere?

Our answer is this: you will not evade desire, the law of presence–absence, the law of the debt, you will find no refuge, not even in action that, far from being a shelter, will expose you more openly than any meditation to the responsibility of naming what needs to be said and done, in other words of recording, hearing and transcribing, at your own risk, the latent meaning of the world 'on which' (as the saying goes) you wish to act.

You can transform this world only by listening to it, and philosophy may appear to be a dead ornament, the pastime of a young lady from a good family (since, like her, it produces no supersonic airplanes or because it works in its room and is of interest to almost nobody), it can be all of that, and is so in reality: the fact remains that it also is, or can be, that moment when the desire within reality comes to itself, when the lack from which we suffer, as individuals or as collectivities, when this lack is named and, by being named, transformed.

But this lack, you will say – is it something

we will ever cease to feel? Does philosophy tell us when, how we can move beyond it? Or, if philosophy knows, as it seems to know these days, that this lack is our law, that all presence is given against a background of absence, then is it not legitimate and reasonable, to despair, to live like dumb beasts? But you won't find any refuge in stupidity either, since it's not that easy to become dumb like a beast; you would need to reject communication and exchange, you would need to obtain absolute silence; and there is no absolute silence, precisely because the world is already speaking, even if confusedly, and you yourself would continue, at least, to dream. And this already says more than enough, when you don't want to hear anything ever again.

So this is why we philosophize: because there is desire, because there is absence in presence, deadness in life; and also because there is our power that is not yet power; and also because there is alienation, the loss of what we thought we had acquired and the gap between the deed and the doing, between the said and the saying; and finally because we cannot evade this: testifying to the presence of the lack with our speech.

In truth, how can we not philosophize?